Samuel Jack Niccolls

The eastern question in prophecy

Six lectures on the rise and decline of Mahometanism

Samuel Jack Niccolls

The eastern question in prophecy
Six lectures on the rise and decline of Mahometanism

ISBN/EAN: 9783337102241

Printed in Europe, USA, Canada, Australia, Japan

Cover: Foto ©Lupo / pixelio.de

More available books at **www.hansebooks.com**

THE
EASTERN QUES[TION]
IN PROPHEC[Y]

SIX LECTURES

ON

THE RISE AND DECLINE OF MAHOMETAN[ISM;]
EVENTS TO FOLLOW, AS PRESENTED
[IN THE PROPHEC]IES OF ST. JOHN,

BY

REV.

PASTOR OF T[HE]

CONTENTS.

LECTURE I.
The Rise of Mahometanism, . 9.

LECTURE II.
The Turkish Power, . 29.

LECTURE III.
The Decline of the Turkish Empire, 47.

LECTURE IV.
The Kings of the East, . 61.

LECTURE V.
Steps Toward the End. 77.

LECTURE VI.
The Millennial Era. . . 95.

PREFACE.

These lectures were not, in the first instance, prepared with a view to publication; and it is owing more to the partial judgment of friends, than to any opinion of my own as to their value, that they now appear in print. I could find no time to re-write them; so they are given to the public in the form in which they were delivered from the pulpit. As they were prepared from week to week, and in the midst of the pressing duties of a city pastorate, there will doubtless be found in them some views and interpretations, which, upon more careful consideration, I would wish to modify. But whatever crudeness of opinion may be found in these pages, I am the more convinced that the views of prophecy presented in them are in the main correct, because they are substantially those held by the wisest and best writers on prophecy. The excellency of any right interpretation of Scripture does not lie in its novelty, but in its truthfulness; and surely it does not argue against its truthfulness that it is old; that it has been presented again and again by careful and faithful students of the Word of God; and that many different minds have reached the same conclusions in their investigations. My aim in preparing these discourses, was to present in as plain and brief a form as possible, what I believed to be the true application of some of the prophecies of St. John, especially with reference to the "Eastern Question." The subject at least, is one of profound interest to all who love the Lord Jesus Christ, and pray for the coming of His kingdom. Statesmen as well as Christians are brought to feel that the world is on the eve of great changes. All look anxiously for what to-morrow shall bring. The present century has already been marked by a most tremendous and significant event,—*the downfall of the Papacy*; or the overthrow of the temporal power of the Pope. If to this shall succeed the overthrow of the "false prophet," the power of Mahometanism, we may well conclude that the world is at the threshold of a new era. All who love truth, and righteousness, and liberty, will rejoice in the speedy overthrow of ecclesiastical despotism, and degrading superstition. Surely then it ought to cause them to lift up their eyes in joyful hope, to learn from the "sure word of prophecy," not only that these "beastly" powers are doomed to destruction, but that the time of their judgment is at hand.

Those who believe the Second Advent of Christ to

be pre-millennial, will object to the views presented in the lecture on the Millennial Era. It is true that the doctrine of the pre-millennial advent of our Lord has been held from the days of the apostles until the present; and that now it is widely advocated by men eminent for their piety and learning. But while at the out-start of my studies, I was strongly disposed to accept it, I must confess that after a careful examination of both sides of the question, it appears to me that the weight of scriptural testimony is on the side of the commonly received doctrine of the Church, which is, that the second coming of Christ in visible glory will be attended by the resurrection of the dead, the final judgment, the end of the world, and the glorification of the Church. The fact of the true, real, and visible coming of our Lord a second time, in glory, is so plainly stated in the Scriptures, that there is no room for doubt or uncertainty. It is the "blessed hope" of the Church. But Christians may honestly differ in their views as to the time and manner of His coming.

If what I have written on this, as well as on other matters of prophecy, will lead any to a careful study of the Word of God, or confirm the faith of those who are doubtful and perplexed, or comfort those who are distressed by the mystery of iniquity, or stir up God's believing children to more exultant hope and abundant labors, I shall count myself rewarded, and thank

God. In the preparation of these discourses I freely acknowledge myself indebted to the labors of others, especially of such scholarly writers as Bengel, Barnes, Hodge, Newton and Cunningham. Regretting the imperfections of my labors, I send this little volume forth, in the hope that what I have written may benefit those who read, and throw across their pathway the glad light that shines from the future, as seen through Jesus Christ, the only Savior of men.

S. J. N.

St. Louis, May, 1877.

Lecture I.

The Rise of Mahometanism.

[Rev. 9: 1—11.]

AND the fifth angel sounded, and I saw a star fall from heaven unto the earth: and to him was given the key of the bottomless pit.

2 And he opened the bottomless pit; and there arose a smoke out of the pit, as the smoke of a great furnace; and the sun and the air were darkened by reason of the smoke of the pit.

3 And there came out of the smoke locusts upon the earth: and unto them was given power, as the scorpions of the earth have power.

4 And it was commanded them that they should not hurt the grass of the earth, neither any green thing, neither any tree; but only those men which have not the seal of God in their foreheads.

5 And to them it was given that they should not kill them, but that they should be tormented five months: and their torment *was* as the torment of a scorpion, when he striketh a man.

6 And in those days shall men seek death, and shall not find it; and shall desire to die, and death shall flee from them.

7 And the shapes of the locusts *were* like unto horses prepared unto battle; and on their heads *were* as it were crowns like gold, and their faces *were* as the faces of men.

8 And they had hair as the hair of women, and their teeth were as *the teeth* of lions.

9 And they had breast-plates, as it were breast-plates of iron; and the sound of their wings *was* as the sound of chariots of many horses running to battle.

10 And they had tails like unto scorpions, and there were stings in their tails: and their power *was* to hurt men five months.

11 And they had a king over them, *which is* the angel of the bottomless pit, whose name in the Hebrew tongue *is* Abaddon, but in the Greek tongue hath *his* name Apollyon.

IN proposing to address you concerning the "Eastern Question," as viewed in the light of prophecy, I do not wish to gratify an idle curiosity; nor yet to lead you away from those great truths of God's Word, which should always be the subject of the pulpit, to mere secular themes. On the contrary, my desire is to confirm your faith in the Scriptures, as a revelation from God, and to show you how all things are guided by our Lord Jesus Christ, for the establishment of His kingdom, and the fulfillment of all the promises He has made.

We as christians, believe and know that all the events of human history, from the migration of a feeble tribe of savages to the overturning of mighty empires, are directed by Him. Confused as earthly affairs may appear to our view, tangled as the threads of history may seem, we know from the Word of God, that there is a clear, definite, and well ordered plan running through all. Just as out of the chaos in the beginning, God brought the well ordered and beautiful cosmos, so now He is building from the confusion of the present, a kingdom of righteousness, and truth and peace, which shall stand forever,—a kingdom that can not be shaken nor pass away. All things move towards the predestined end; all yield and work together under that mighty power, whereby He is able to subdue all things unto Himself.

For this reason all of the movements of the present, as well as the events of the past, have a peculiar interest for the believer. He looks at them, not as a politician or a statesman, but as a member of that kingdom in whose behalf they are working. With each passing event, no matter whether full of glory or terror, he can lift up his head with joyful confidence, for he knows that redemption draws nigh. Wars and revolutions are to him the echoes of the footfalls of the coming King of Glory. While this is true in general of the whole course of history, there are certain events which have a special interest to christians, because they have been predicted by the Word of God. They are like great headlands and lighthouses marked down on a chart, which, when they come in view after long leagues of sailing over wastes of water, assure the voyager that he is on the right course to the desired haven.

For the comfort and encouragement of His people, the Lord Jesus revealed under the new dispensation, as under the old, certain great events in the future, which when seen in history would be recognized as the fulfillment of His word, and as landmarks by the way. These events are so revealed, that they can be recognized with certainty only when they come to pass; but they are also so revealed in their general character, as to lead us to look in the direction in which they shall appear, and to awaken the confident expectation of their coming to pass. With this sure word of prophecy in our hands, we are like a company of voyagers at sea examining their chart. The vessel is enshrouded with fog; no sun is seen overhead; no stars give their friendly light to help conjecture as to the course. Still, the vessel under skillful guidance has kept on her way. From the chart they conjecture that they ought to be near such a headland and lighthouse. Some are confident that they at last see them;—but what seemed like a shore turns out to be a bank of clouds; and what they thought was the shining of the lantern from the lighthouse, proves to be the light from a vessel befogged like their own. But in due time the skillful captain who is not misled nor deceived, brings them in full view of the real headland and lighthouse, and the chart by which they had sailed, is confirmed. So here, special events are predicted, that when they do come to pass, we may know that our course is homeward to the desired haven.

One of these prophetical events, as we gather from the Divine chart, is now before us. We know the general direction in which to look for it, and, in the main, its character; but in our eagerness and ignorance we may mistake something else for it; we may cry too soon, "lo! there it is!" and a nearer view show that to be a cloud, which fancy called a reality. But certain it is, that in the fullness of time the unerring Captain, who guides all, shall bring us in sight of it; and men shall say, "it has come to pass according to the word of the Lord."

But what is it that we are to expect? Can we so learn the order of events from the divine plan, as to declare with confidence what next shall appear in the succession of landmarks?

There has now come before the world what is called "the Eastern Question." It is evidently of no small importance, for it agitates the courts and cabinets of all Europe. It is not a new question, for ever since the time of the Crusades, it has been vexing Europe; it has already cost millions of lives and untold treasures. In spite of all treaties and compromises, it again appears before the world, demanding a solution. Why is it that all eyes are looking in the same direction? What concentrates so much interest about a certain territory in the East? This question locates itself in a region that has comparatively little to make it desirable in the way of wealth and commerce. Ages of misrule and oppression have ruined the land that was once the seat of the world's empire; and its inhabitants are wretched and degraded indeed. But most significantly it involves the future of the land of promise and prophecy,—the fate of Constantinople and the Turks involves the destiny of Palestine. Give England or France the Holy Land, and it is a matter of comparative indifference who rules at Constantinople. Palestine is the key to the whole position. The region between the Euphrates and the Nile, occupying such a remarkable position in the history of the past, and in the development of God's purposes with men, again rises as a central point in human affairs. Across it lies the future pathway of the world's trade. It is the road to the distant East. The power that acquires it, whether it be England, France or Russia, has the Gibraltar of Asia, and is for the time mistress of the world.

This question not only touches the land of prophecy, but it also concerns the nation of prophecy,—that peculiar people who for eighteen centuries have been an anomaly in the world's history, and who without a country and wandering in all lands as in exile, have witnessed the rise and fall of nations and empires, and yet remain imperishable in their sorrow. How comes it that expectation is alive among them, and busy rumor speaks of their return to the land of Abraham and David? Men may account for all this simply on the ground of natural feeling and ambition; they may look at it as a question involving "the balance of power," or stirred up by the rivalry of nations: but one thing all agree in—it is full of tremendous results, and its solution will mark an era in history.

In viewing this subject in the light of prophecy, let me say, once for all, that while prophecy is sure, man's application of it is not. Men have made many false interpretations of it, and will still make them through ignorance or design. It becomes him who would interpret it, to do it with humility and honesty. A minister in applying it, cannot always speak with the same positive confidence, as when he warns sinners of the wrath to come, and proclaims the necessity of faith in Christ in order to salvation.

It is not for us to know the times and seasons beforehand, with arithmetical accuracy, lest faith should be lost in sight, and the discipline of waiting, and hope, and limitation be lost to us. There was a world of good sense in the homely advice of an old Scotchman to his pastor, who had announced a series of lectures on the Revelation, "Trot along minister among the seven churches, but when you come to the seals and trumpets drive canny." Let us try to find out what is certain and reasonable, and not venture beyond our depth in unknown things.

(1.) In the Revelation, we have what is admitted by all christians, to be a prophetic account of the future of the church of God, from the age of the writer until the glorious end of redemption. Part of this revelation is confirmed by the testimony of the ancient prophets, and especially by Daniel. Part of it is already verified by history,—enough at least, to confirm every candid reader, both of history and of this Book, in the belief that all that remains unfulfilled of St. John's prophecies, shall certainly come to pass.

(2.) In this revelation we have an order of events described. As for example, there is the opening of the "seals" in their order: there is the sounding of the "trumpets" in their order. These manifestly signify certain events, or rather periods in which certain events come to pass. We know also that there is an order of events in history. Now if we can take this book of prophecy, and placing it along side the book of history, find that the order of events and the description of them as given in each book, agree one with the other, surely we are justified in saying not only that the prophecy is true, but also, that what remains in it, as yet unfulfilled, will come to pass in the order and manner described. This is what I propose to do with this "Eastern Question:"—take the facts of history and place them along side the prophecy; and then you must judge for yourselves as to the correspondence. In doing this, you will be able also to draw conclusions as to the way in which the remaining part of the predictions is to be fulfilled. We might proceed to take up immediately, that part of the Revelation which, as all biblical scholars affirm, applies to the Mahometan power in the East, and from it, attempt to forecast the issue of the present struggle. But it is only when we come to see that this part of the prophecy is one of a series preceding it, which has already had its fulfillment in history, that what by the first method would only be a plausible interpretation, becomes a settled conviction.

The best interpretation of prophecy is that made in the light of its past fulfillment. Our wisest course then, is to trace the "Eastern Question" from the beginning.

In the ninth chapter of the Revelation, we have the record of the sounding of the fifth trumpet heralding a new judgment that was to come upon the earth. What followed is described in the language of symbols: it must be remembered too, that as St. John employs Old Testament or biblical imagery, we are to find the meaning of his symbols and figures within the Bible and not outside of it.

"*I saw a star fall from heaven unto the earth.*" A "star" is the emblem of a religious teacher and ruler. Thus in the prophecy of Balaam we read,—"a star shall come out of Jacob, and a sceptre shall rise out of Israel." The ministers of the seven churches are represented by stars—Rev. 1: 20. Jesus Christ is the "bright and morning star;" the one that leads and outshines all the rest. But in this case the prophet sees a "falling star" or meteor,—the striking symbol of the brilliant and destructive career of some great false teacher and leader. Its origin seemed to be in the heavens among the stars, but after all, it was earth born; its brilliant pathway through the skies created wonder and admiration, and enkindled superstitious awe and terror,—but, at last it vanished in the earth. Its ignoble end proclaimed its true nature. "*To him was given the key of the bottomless pit;*" that is, of the abode of the powers of evil and darkness. Mark the expression, "was given;"—the key was not his by right, but in the development of God's purpose he was to use it. The powers of darkness are under the divine control, nor can they rage or go forth to destroy save as God permits. In his providential government He suffers the rise of wicked men into power, and the unloosing of the forces of hell, as a judgment upon men for their impenitency and unbelief. "*He opened the bottomless pit.*" This declares the mission of the one symbolized by the meteor, to be chiefly that of a false religious teacher. Through his instrumentality, a new delusion, brought about not by perverting existing truths, but as it were, direct from the bottomless pit, is to come forth among men. His was not the blessed work of binding the powers of darkness, but rather, to unloose them, and so prepare the way for a flood of error to cover the world. "*And there arose smoke out of the pit, as the smoke of a great furnace.*" Here we have the apt emblem of religious error or a false revelation. It is something that darkens the "air" and the "sun." It shuts out the older and divine light, "the sun," by perverting the very medium, "the air," through which men receive it. It is a revelation from the pit such as hell might well delight in. It is also, evidently an error of great power, spreading far and wide; it rises as "the smoke of a great furnace." Gen. 19: 28. Out of this "smoke" came "*locusts upon the earth.*" This is the symbol of something visible and tangible: they are born out of the smoke; created and animated by this error from the pit. It was customary with the prophets to compare a vast invading host, to those swarms of locusts so common and so dreaded in the east. Nah. 3: 16. Joel. 2: 4, 5.

As we read the description here given by St. John, we cannot doubt that it is the picture of a vast horde or host of warriors going forth on their mission of conquest. The symbol employed, not only locates the field of their conquests in the East, the region of the locusts, but it also suggests the country from which they come. Arabia was the home of the locusts, and the people of the east associated them with that region, just as we do oranges with the south, or grasshoppers with the plains. The sceptical Volney whose writings Gibbon praises so highly, says, "the inhabitants of Syria have remarked that locusts came constantly from the desert of Arabia." In Arabian writings the locust is introduced as the national emblem of the Ishmaelites. The warriors described in the vision are like locusts as to their origin, their multitude and the manner of their going forth. But there are two remarkable exceptions. "*It was commanded them that they should not hurt the grass of the earth, neither any green thing, neither any tree.*" Men are their prey. "*And they had a king over them.*" The very reverse of this is true of the ordinary locusts:—Prov. 30: 27. They were "*like unto horses prepared for battle.*" This at once suggests the idea of a vast body of cavalry going forth to war. They wore on their heads, "*as it were, crowns like gold:*" it is literally "diadems." Locusts are bald: but these were distinguished by a peculiar headdress which appeared like a diadem of a yellow or golden color. Their power to torment and plague was limited to "*five months:*" that is according to the usual method of reckoning prophetic times, a period of one hundred and fifty years.

There are many interesting and suggestive details in this vision, which the present time will not permit us to consider; but in view of what has been said, it will readily be admitted that St. John foresees the rise and mission of some great invading and conquering host, animated by a false religion. He points out the country from which it comes; he describes its movements, the personal appearance of the warriors, their dress, their manner of action, their mission, their rule. and the duration of their conquering career.

With this description in our hands, we ought surely to be able to identify the reality, if it has already appeared in human affairs. Let us then turn to the pages of history to see if we can find there, any power which can be fairly indentified as the army of "the locusts," predicted by St. John. Fortunately there is at hand. accessible to all, a history whose authority as a standard all admit, and to whose testimony in this case not even the most sceptical can object. It is a monument of learning and careful research, and in its fascinating pages will be found the most striking commentary on parts of the Revelation ever written. Certainly no one will accuse it of partiality to Christianity, or say that it was written designedly in the interests of New Testament prophecy. It is Gibbon's history of the Decline and Fall of the Roman Empire. Its learned author delights in sneering at the christian faith, and even when he records with unquestionable truthfulness the vices and superstitions that corrupted the Church, he does it with an ill-concealed gratification. But after all, it seems as if this sneering infidel was raised up to be an unconscious witness to the truth of God's Word; and that like Balaam of old, though he meant to curse, he has ended in confirming the testimony of the God of Israel. From the brilliant pages of his history, I take the facts which I desire to place along side this prophecy, for the purpose of identification.

In the history of the first six centuries of the Christian era, nothing can be found that adequately fulfills the prophecy which we have been considering. But in the opening of the seventh century, a great movement begins in Arabia, so extraordinary in its character, methods and results, as to recall to the thoughtful reader of the Bible. St. John's vision of the army of the locusts. It was in the year A. D. 571, that Mahomet was born. To this marvelous man was given the power to establish a new religion, which speedily overturned the altars of Christianity in Asia and Africa. No better emblem of his career can be found, than that of a meteor suddenly appearing in the heavens. exciting wonder and awe by its brilliant course, and then disappearing in the earth. He came, claiming to be the prophet of God—a divine leader and teacher of men. Gibbon writes: "In the cave of Hera, three miles from Mecca, he consulted the spirit of fraud and enthusiasm whose abode is not in the heavens, but in the mind of the prophet. The faith which under the name of Islam, he preached to his family and nation. is compounded of an eternal truth and a necessary fiction,—that there is only one God, and that Mahomet is the apostle of God."

He stands forth pre-eminently as the false prophet of the Christian centuries; and still, after the lapse of twelve hundred years, he is revered by millions as the apostle of God. The Koran, a strange mixture of imposture and fanaticism, of Arabian and Jewish traditions, of speculations, and truths taken from the Scriptures, in a comparatively brief space of time became the accepted revelation of God, to at least the third part of the then known world. Like "smoke" filling the air, it darkened the minds of men and shut out the true light of the Divine Word. It was indeed a revelation from the pit of darkness, a representation of the living God, and of the truth necessary for salvation that well might have been conceived in hell, in order to destroy the souls of men. If the historian of the present, were to search for an emblem to describe the mental and spiritual condition of those who accept the Koran, he could find nothing more appropriate than to say "that they are covered with a cloud of smoke that shuts out all true light."

Under the teachings and inspiration of this new faith, grew up those formidable bands of armed fanatics, who came from Arabia to spread themselves like swarms of locusts over the Eastern World. Gibbon describes those who flocked to the banner of the false prophet, allured by the prospect of conquest and plunder, or compelled by the sword, as "myriads." These hosts of bearded and turbaned horsemen, known as the Saracens, passing rapidly to and fro, as though carried on wings, were irresistible in their power. "In ten years of the administration of Omar, they reduced to his obedience 3600 cities and castles, destroyed 4000 churches, and built 4000 mosques. One hundred years after the flight of Mahomet from Mecca, the reign of his successors extended from India to the Atlantic Ocean. Persia, Syria, Egypt, Africa and Spain were subject to their authority." The historian has carefully recorded certain peculiarities about the movements of these armies of Islamism, which are most significant when placed along side the picture drawn by St. John. Unlike other conquerers of the Eastern World, where ever they went, they forced upon the people the deadly error of their new faith. The nation that fell under their power was as one stung with "a scorpion;" the deadly poison of Mahometanism was infused into its veins. "*Their torment was as the torment of a scorpion when he striketh a man.*" How aptly does this set forth the condition of the people who have been poisoned by the teachings of the Koran.

Another feature in the conquests of the Saracens was so strange and unlike all the methods of all previous invasions, that the historian dwells upon it at length. One of the precepts of Mahomet forbade his followers from destroying any fruit trees or gardens or vineyards, in the region which they attempted to conquer. When Abubeker led forth the army destined for the conquest of Syria, he gave these orders: "Remember that you are always in the presence of God, on the verge of death, in the assurance of judgment, and the hope of paradise. When you fight the battles of the Lord, acquit yourselves like men, without turning your backs, destroy no palm trees, nor any fields of corn, cut down no fruit trees, nor do any mischief to cattle, only such as you kill to eat."—(Gibbon.) Such were the marching orders of the Saracens, and they were strictly and religiously observed in all their invasions. This refraining from destroying orchards and vineyards, and fields of corn, was as strange a feature in war, as then conducted, as though vast swarms of locusts should light upon the earth, and pass over it and yet not hurt or devour any green thing. But if we turn to the prophecy, we will find that this singular characteristic is not overlooked—"*And it was commanded them that they should not hurt the grass of the earth, neither any green thing, neither any tree.*"

The religious zeal of the Saracens was directed especially against those whom they esteemed idolaters. In this class they reckoned those professed christians who worshipped images and relics, and paid divine honors to saints and angels. But history records the fact that those parts of the christian church, which in the midst of abounding corruption adhered to the ancient scriptural faith, were most singularly preserved from Mahometan violence. This was the case with the Nestorians in the East; although dwelling in countries under the rule of the Saracens, they were comparatively unmolested in their worship. Abubeker's orders to his armies were; "As you go on you will find some religious people who live retired in monasteries and propose to themselves to serve God in that way: let them alone, and neither kill them, nor destroy their monasteries: and you will find another sort of people, that belong to the synagogue of Satan, who have shaven crowns: be sure you cleave their skulls, and give them no quarter until they either turn Mahometans or pay tribute." Equally remarkable was the preservation of true Christianity in the heart of Europe. After the Saracens had completed the conquest of Spain and Portugal, they intended to make a descent on Italy, and thus complete the conquest of Europe. But fortunately for the cause of humanity and Christian civilization, this purpose was frustrated by the valor of Charles Martel. A successful battle arrested the tide of invasion, which, had it swept over the Alps, would have changed the destinies of the world. It has often been remarked, that the arrest of the Saracen hosts before Europe was subdued, was what there was no reason to anticipate, and it even yet perplexes historians to account for it. Hallam in his History of the Middle Ages, says; "these conquests which astonish the careless and superficial, are less perplexing to a calm inquirer, than their cessation—the loss of half the Roman Empire, than the preservation of the rest." But is there not in all. this. the verification of this declaration"? *It was commanded them that they should not hurt the grass of the earth, but only those men which have not the seal of God in their foreheads."* They were raised up as a plague upon apostate Christendom, but not to destroy the true church of Christ.

Another striking characteristic of the Saracen soldiers, was their desire for death. So filled were they with the fanatical doctrines of the Koran, that they actually sought death on the field of battle, in order to be translated speedily to Paradise. "The sword," said Mahomet, "is the key of heaven and of hell; a drop of blood shed in the cause of God, a night spent in arms, are of more avail than two months of fasting and prayer; whosoever falls in battle, his sins are forgiven; at the day of judgment his wounds shall be resplendent as vermillion, and as odoriferous as musk; the loss of his limbs shall be supplied by the wings of angels and cherubims." "By such revelations," Gibbon remarks, "the souls of the Arabs were filled with enthusiasm; the picture of the invisible world was strongly painted on their imaginations, and death, which they had always despised, became an object of hope and desire." They rushed to battle as to a feast, crying, "Fight, fight! Paradise, paradise!" Turn from these words of the historian to those of the revelator: *"And in these days shall men seek death, and shall not find it: and shall desire to die, and death shall flee from them."*

This same historian informs us concerning the duration of the Saracen conquests. From the time Mahomet preached his first crusade in Mecca, A. D. 612, until A. D. 762, when Caliph Almansor built Bagdad and called it "the city of peace," is a period of 150 years. After this time they made no further encroachments upon Christendom. "War" says Gibbon, "was now no longer the passion of the Saracens: there, the luxury of the Caliphs relaxed the nerves, and terminated the progress of the Arabian empire." This corresponds precisely with the prophetic period of *five months*, or 150 years, during which they were to be a torment to Christendom. *"And their power was to hurt men five months."*

Still another peculiarity of the Saracen rule is, that during all its existence it was as though *one man reigned*. Mahomet lived and ruled in his successors. The Caliphs professed to derive their authority from him, and to govern according to his laws. Gibbon writes; "the regal and sacerdotal characters were united in the successors of Mahomet: and if the Koran was the rule of their actions, they were the supreme judges and interpreters of that divine book." Here also, the correspondence with the language of St. John is perfect. *"And they had a king over them which is the angel of the bottomless pit*, (that is the one mentioned in the first verse, as having the key of the pit,) *whose* name in the Hebrew tongue is *Abaddon*, but in the Greek tongue hath his name *Apollyon*," that is "destroyer." And how fitting the title for him, whose mission it was to set up and leave behind him a religion that has cursed the bodies and souls of millions, for ages!

Other points might readily be noticed in the history, which would explain and confirm the description given in the prophecy; but without dwelling upon these, let us notice in conclusion, the effects of the conquests of the Saracens as presented in history and prophecy.

The Saracen invasions swept over those parts of the world in which Christianity had first been planted, and where it had been in the course of time, most deeply corrupted by superstition and philosophy. Indeed, the whole force and aim of this new power of Islamism were so manifestly directed against the church as then existing, that it was regarded as the plague and woe of Christendom. The Christian empire trembled before it, and at times it seemed to human view, as if the crescent was destined to supplant the cross, and the Koran, instead of the Scriptures, shape the thought and religion of Europe. And certainly the condition of the church then, was such as to invite and justify this judgment. Gibbon writes, "the Christians of the seventh century insensibly relapsed into a semblance of paganism: their public and private vows were addressed to the relics and images that disgraced the temples of the East. The throne of the Almighty was darkened by a crowd of martyrs, and saints and angels, the objects of popular veneration." And again he writes: "The use, and even the worship of images, was firmly established before the end of the sixth century." But instead of repenting in view of the judgments which had overwhelmed the Eastern churches, the remainder held fast to their superstitious and idolatrous rites, and the number of saints to whom adoration was paid, increased instead of diminished.

All this corresponds precisely with the language of St. John, both as to the cause of this "woe" and its effects upon a degenerate church—"*And the rest of the men which were not killed by these plagues, yet repented not of the works of their hands, that they should not worship devils* (i. e. demons, or the disembodied souls of men) *and idols of gold, and silver, and brass, and stone, and of wood.*"

So far then, the identification is complete. The Word of God has pointed out to us the rise and first stages of that power, which still lives to vex and trouble the nations; and upon whose utter overthrow so much that is glorious in the future, depends. And surely, if the minute description of its rise and first mission, made five hundred years before it came into existence, has been literally fulfilled, we may rightly expect the remaining part of the prediction to come to pass according to the Word of the Lord.

But while we reflect upon this omniscience of God as revealed in prophecy, and upon his faithfulness to his word as revealed in history, let us not forget what He has declared concerning our own personal future. We may read our destiny in the light of His promises. He who fulfills His word among the nations, also keeps covenant with them that trust in Him. "He that believeth on the Son hath everlasting life. And he that believeth not the Son shall not see life but the wrath of

God abideth on him." Do not expect that the future will in any way falsify this declaration. Shall God keep His word to the nations and yet break it to individuals? Take heed then I beseech you, to the word which He has spoken to you, my hearer. The "question" which most of all should concern you, is not one to be solved in the distant "East;" but it is one close at hand, and to be determined in your own heart:—HAVE YOU BELIEVED ON THE LORD JESUS CHRIST?

"That Holy One,
Who came to earth for Thee,—
Oh, strangest thing beneath the Sun,
That He, by any mortal one,
Forgotten e'er should be!

The Son of God,
Who pity had on Thee;
Who turned aside the smiting rod.
And all alone the Garden trod,—
Forgotten shall He be?"

Lecture II.

The Turkish Power.

[Rev. 9: 12-21.]

ONE woe is past: *and* behold, there come two woes more hereafter.
13 And the sixth angel sounded, and I heard a voice from the four horns of the golden altar which is before God,
14 Saying to the sixth angel which had the trumpet, Loose the four angels which are bound in the great river Euphrates.
15 And the four angels were loosed, which were prepared for an hour, and a day, and a month, and a year, for to slay the third part of men.
16 And the number of the army of the horsemen *were* two hundred thousand thousand: and I heard the number of them.
17 And thus I saw horses in the vision, and them that sat on them, having breast plates of fire, and of jacinth, and brimstone: and the heads of the horses *were* as the heads of lions; and out of their mouths issued fire, and smoke, and brimstone.
18 By these three was the third part of men killed, by the fire, and by the smoke, and by the brimstone, which issued out of their mouths.
19 For their power is in their mouth, and in their tails: for their tails *were* like unto serpents, and had heads, and with them do they hurt.
20 And the rest of the men which were not killed by these plagues, yet repented not of the works of their hands, that they should not worship devils, and idols of gold, and silver, and brass, and stone, and of wood: which neither can see, nor hear, nor walk;
21 Neither repented they of their murders, nor of their sorceries, nor of their fornication, nor of their thefts.

ON last Sabbath evening, your attention was called to the prophetic events following the sounding of the fifth trumpet. These, as was shown to you, found their fulfillment in the rise of Mahometanism, and in the empire of the Saracens. Immediately following this in the prophetic series, is the announcement of another "woe" heralded by the sounding of the sixth trumpet. "*And the sixth angel sounded, and I heard a voice from the four horns of the golden altar which is before God.*"

Here we have described the divine source of this coming judgment. As the symbols by which the revelator describes heavenly things are taken from the Old Testament, we can readily understand what is symbolized by "the golden altar." It was the altar of incense standing before the Most Holy Place, in the temple: on it was burnt the sweet spices whose ascending fragrance represented the prayers of God's people, always acceptable in his sight when offered through the mediation of Jesus Christ. It is from the "golden altar," that is in answer to the cries of His praying people, that the Voice comes which commands preparation for further judgments upon the earth. Jesus Christ in encouraging men to pray, says,—"and shall not God avenge his own elect, which cry day and night unto Him, though He bear long with them? I tell you that He will avenge them speedily." Here, as a confirmation to His own words, He draws aside the vail, and shows us how the stupendous events of history work in the interests of those, who by faith lay hold of the horns of the golden altar that is before God. Yes, prayer is a power in the world. Kings and statesmen may take counsel together, and marshal the forces of empires, but over all is One who listens at the "golden altar" for the cries of His people, and in due time, His voice will be heard espousing their cause, and calling for judgment upon their enemies.

The Divine Voice commands a messenger "*To loose the four angels which are bound in the great river Euphrates.*" This points us to the earthly origin of the coming "woe." It takes its rise in the general region of which the Euphrates is the chief river. It is customary, not only with the prophetical writers, but also in modern language, to designate certain regions by one or more of their characteristic natural features. As for example, we speak of the valley of the Mississippi, or the land of the Nile; each of these great rivers being the most prominent natural feature in its respective region. We can readily gather from the prophecy that the power which is to come forth from the old Babylonian empire, is to be a military host of vast numbers. "*The number of the army of the horsemen was two hundred thousand thousand.*" Here we have a definite number put to represent the indefinite number of a great host. The revelator says he "*heard the number of them.*" He did not see all of them, thus indicating that they do not all appear at once, in one army, but through a succession of years. The time of their mission of destruction is given. "*They were made ready for an hour, and a day, and a month, and a year.*" Reckoning each "day" to stand for a year of 360 days, this would represent a period of 391 years, and the part of a year indicated by "an hour,"—that is the twelfth, or twenty-fourth part of 360 days. This method of dividing the year into twelve equal parts of thirty days each, is as old as the time of Noah, and possibly was the primitive year; but when intercalation was necessary, an additional month was added. So we may regard these prophetic years as equivalent to the same number of ordinary years. In this period, the "four angels" of the Euphrates, "*were to slay the third part of men*" Under the fifth trumpet, the hosts represented by the locusts were not to kill men, but to torment them. Accordingly we found that the

Saracens, while overrunning and subduing the Christian Empire in Spain, Africa, Egypt, and all Asia, with the exception of a small portion of territory between the Mediterranean and Black Sea, still spared the larger portion of nominal Christians, though their lot was one of terrible oppression and distress. But this new hostile power is to stand in a different relation to Christendom. It is to be a "slayer," rather than a tormentor.

It is further described, as "the four angels which are bound." All forces or agencies may be used as God's "angels" or "messengers," for so the word means. Fire and hail, snow and vapor, and stormy winds fulfill His Word. He may send the hornets, as in Canaan, or command the destructive elements of flood and fire, or marshal invading armies to execute His righteous judgments. The number "four" is the number of totality or completeness. Thus "the four corners of the earth" represent the whole earth. Is. 11: 12; The "four winds," all the winds from every side. Math. 25: 31. So also the completeness of heaven is represented by describing it as "four square" Rev. 21: 16. By the "four angels," then, we are to understand all the power to the full extent, which for a time had been bound in the region represented by the Euphrates. We know from what follows, that it is a military power, especially of horsemen or cavalry. In the 17th and 19th verses we have a description of their appearance, and manner of warfare. Bright colors of red and blue and yellow, characterize their dress. The method of their warfare is also strikingly different from that of the hosts under the fifth trumpet, though they also were horsemen. "*Out of their mouths issued fire, and smoke, and brimstone."* Some new, wonderful and exceedingly destructive agency, is used by them in their conquests.

Let us now lay the prophetical picture along side of written history, and see if we can discover its counterpart. We found in the former lecture, that the events described under the fifth trumpet, were not all realized in history until the eighth century; so we need not look earlier than that period for the fulfillment of what is here described. It is declared, "one woe is past; behold there come two woes more hereafter."

The vision itself, points us to the Euphrates, so that we are at no loss as to what portion of history we must search to find its fulfillment, if it has been realized. Again we turn to Gibbon, whose fascinating pages picture so graphically the rise and fall of empires in the East. The Saracens after their rapid and wonderful career of conquest, built their capital, the city of Bagdad, in the region of the Euphrates. There the Caliphs, the proud successors of Mahomet, lived in luxury, and cultivated peace. The throne of Mahometanism was transported from the deserts of Arabia to the fertile plains of Mesopotamia. But soon this mighty Empire felt the power of that law of decay, from which no nation has ever been able to escape. In the tenth century, its glory was gone. Peace had brought luxury; and luxury, licentiousness and decay. From A. D. 770 to A. D. 1040, this mighty power of Islamism, which once threatened the destruction of Christendom, made no conquests. It was "bound" in the region of the Euphrates. Faction rose against faction; wars and tumults, and assassinations followed each other in rapid succession. The old Empire was in ruins and a new builder was needed. In due time, the next actor in this strange scene of strife and judgment appears. East of the Caspian Sea, and north of the ancient empire of Persia, is a region of country called on our maps, Turkestan. This was the original seat of the Turks or Turkmans. They were the ancient Scythians of the sixth century, and their name was still famous among the Greeks and Orientals for their fierceness, courage, and cruelty in war. While the Empire of the Caliphs was falling to pieces, these wild shepherds and horsemen of the North descended in vast hordes upon the kingdom of Persia, and in course of a comparatively short period, erected a splendid and solid empire, extending from the river Indus, to the confines of Greece and Egypt: nor did they cease in their victorious career, until the crescent had displaced the cross on the dome of St. Sophia, and the capital of the old Roman World became their seat of empire. One of the greatest of the Turkish princes was Mahmud, who reigned in Persia 1000 years after the birth of Christ. For him the title of Sultan, meaning "lord" or "master," was first invented. As to the number of these armed bands that swept down year after year to spread themselves over the plains of Persia, Gibbon makes this statement—"The Sultan had inquired of one of the chiefs, what supply of men he could furnish for military service. 'If you send,' replied Ismael, 'one of these arrows into our camp, 50,000 of your servants will mount on horseback.'—'And if that number should not be sufficient?'—'Send this second arrow to the horde of Balik, and you will find 50,000 more.' 'But' said the Sultan, 'if I should stand in need of the whole force of your kindred tribes?'—'Dispatch my bow,' was the last reply of Ismael, 'and the summons will be obeyed by 200,000 horse.'"

The whole body of the Turkish nation embraced the religion of Mahomet with fervor and sincerity, and with their relentless cimeters, they became the most zealous and successful of missionaries. In their career of conquest, they enthroned themselves in Bagdad, the capital of Mahometanism and the seat of the Caliphs, and at that place, their great leader, Togrul, was solemnly proclaimed to be lieutenant of the vicar of Mahomet, and the Commander of the armies of the Faithful. This significant event occurred A. D. 1058. The "preparation" in the divine purpose was now complete; the thunderbolt was forged which was to fall in judgment upon apostate Christendom. The time for "loosing" the powers of the Euphrates had come. About four years after his solemn enthronement at Bagdad, Togrul led his armies against the Grecian or Roman Empire, and began that long and bloody contest which for nearly four centuries kept Europe in excitement, anxiety and terror, and cost the lives of millions of her people. At the head of his horsemen, Togrul crossed the Euphrates, and the first campaign of this new invasion is thus described by the historian: "the myriads of Turkish horsemen overspread a frontier of six hundred miles, and the blood of 130,000 Christians was a grateful sacrifice to the Arabian Prophet." After this, for a time it seemed as if this tide of destruction had receded, to rise no more; but it came again with its destroying floods.

At the death of Malek Shah, one of the successors of Togrul, the Turkish Empire was broken into four parts. This separation was lasting. At first, following the usual course of factions, their arms were turned against each other. But once when their armies were in battle array expecting the signal, the Caliph, the successor of Mahomet, forgetful of the majesty which secluded him from vulgar eyes, interposed his mediation. "Instead of shedding the blood of your brethren, brethren both in descent and in faith, unite your forces in a holy war against the Greeks, the enemies of God and His Apostle." They listened to his voice; and the eldest of the rival leaders, the valiant Soliman, accepted the royal standard which gave him the free conquest and hereditary command of the provinces of the Roman Empire. from Arzeroum to Constantinople and the unknown regions of the West. Accompanied by his four brothers he passed the Euphrates, and the Turkish camp was soon seated in the neighborhood of Kutaieh in Phrygia." Now began a series of lasting conquests over the Christian empire, which did not cease until after the taking of Constantinople, in A. D. 1453. With the fall of the Imperial city, the supremacy of the Turks was fully established in the East; and Christianity was almost exterminated in the countries of its birth-place and early triumphs. From the time that Togrul started from Bagdad about A. D. 1060, to A. D. 1453, is a period of 391 years, the time specified for this "woe" by the prophet. Here, were the dates in history sufficiently accurate, we might be able to verify the prophecy to the fraction of the year.

Thus the time of the rise of the Turkish power corresponds with the predictions of St. John. But can we find in history, the fulfillment of their prophetic mission during this period,—"to slay the third part of men?" The history of Turkish conquests is indeed a bloody one. For three hundred and fifty years, their record is little else than that of an invading army and a hostile camp among the nations. The names of Saladin, Soliman, Zengis-Khan, Othman, Bajazet, Tamerlane, Mahomet II, and a host of others, at once suggest scenes of rapine and slaughter, and remind us of careers marked with the bleaching bones of countless victims. The remains of the Christian empire in Asia were soon trodden to the dust under the hoofs of their horsemen. The churches which had been spared under the oppressive toleration of the Saracens, were literally exterminated by the Turks. In the first assault against the Christian provinces in Asia Minor, 130,000 victims fell under their cimeters: at Antioch, where the disciples were first called Christians, the church that Paul had indoctrinated was entirely destroyed.

At Nice, where the famous council of the Catholic church had proclaimed in unmistakable language the doctrine of the divinity of Jesus Christ, these followers of the false prophet established for a time their capital, and derided the name of Jesus in the churches that once echoed with hymns to his praise. Under them the captivity and ruin of the seven churches of Asia, to which St. John addresses the solemn admonitions in the opening of his prophecies, were consummated. In the second and third chapters of the Revelation, we find that all these churches, with the single exception of the one in Philadelphia, were threatened with destruction. Concerning the latter, the following prediction was made:—"Behold, I will make them of the synagogue of Satan, which say they are Jews and are not, but do lie; behold, I will make them to come and worship before thy feet, and to know that I have loved thee. Because thou hast kept the word of my patience, I also will keep thee from the hour of temptation, which shall come upon all the world, to try them that dwell upon the earth." Rev. 3: 9—10. Now turn to the pages of Gibbon and see the record of history.

"The ruin of the seven churches of Asia was consummated: and the barbarous lords of Ionia and Lydia still trample on the monuments of classic and Christian antiquity. In the loss of Ephesus, the Christians deplored the fall of the first 'angel,' the extinction of the 'first candlestick' of the Revelation. The desolation is complete. The circus and three stately theatres of Laodicea are now peopled with wolves and foxes: Sardis is reduced to a miserable village; the God of Mahomet without a rival or a son, is invoked in the mosques of Thyatira and Pergamos. Philadelphia alone has been saved by prophecy or courage. At a distance from the sea, forgotten by the emperors, encompassed on all sides by the Turks, her valiant citizens defended their religion above four-score years. Among the Greek colonies and churches of Asia, Philadelphia is still erect, a column in a scene of ruins, a pleasing example that the paths of honor and safety may sometimes be the same." How strikingly do the words of the sceptical historian echo the language of the Spirit: "Because thou hast kept the word of my patience, I also will keep thee from the hour of temptation."

Crossing into Europe, the victorious Turks speedily overran all that remained of the Greek empire. On the plains of Servia, where this old contest threatens to break out anew, they defeated the great armies that Europe marshalled against them, with tremendous slaughter, and extended their conquests to the gates of Vienna. One of their Sultans, from a victorious battle field, threatened to feed his horse from the altar of St. Peter at Rome; and such was the terror of Europe before his arms, that only a fit of gout prevented the accomplishment of his threat.

Constantinople, for ages the seat of the Christian emperors, at last fell into their power, and the crescent was victorious over the cross throughout the Eastern World. But this long history of bloody and relentless war against the Christians does not measure the extent of Turkish slaughters. About the same time that these powers from the Euphrates were "loosed to slay the third part of men," there began in Europe that wonderful movement, known in history as the crusades. Under the reign of the Saracens, the spirit of toleration permitted the Christians of Europe to visit the city made sacred by the death and resurrection of the Redeemer of men. But when the Turks occupied Jerusalem, "a spirit of native barbarism, or recent zeal, prompted them to insult the clergy of every sect; the patriarch was dragged by the hair along the pavement and cast into a dungeon; divine worship in the church of the Resurrection was often disturbed by the savage rudeness of its masters." The pathetic tale of the indignities which the Christian pilgrims suffered, excited the millions of the West to march under the standard of the cross to the relief of the Holy Land. The historian significantly writes:—"a nerve was touched of exquisite feeling, and the sensation vibrated to the heart of Europe." In A. D. 1095, Pope Urban proclaimed the first crusade. Thus began the great religious war, which according to the testimony of history—"almost depopulated Europe." It was carried on during a period of two hundred years, and more than two millions of Christians were sacrificed in the seven crusades. So great was the enthusiasm in this movement, that the East was threatened with a wholesale migration from the West. Emperors, kings, bishops, priests, monks, nuns, and even multitudes of women and children joined the hosts of the crusaders, and were carried to the land of the Turks, as by a great tide, only to be slaughtered. It seemed as if in their own land the Turks stood as executioners, the divinely appointed slayers of men, and the people of Europe pressed on in a ceaseless stream to their execution. "Six succeeding generations" says the historian, "rushed headlong down the precipice that was open before them. In a period of two centuries after the council of Clermont, each spring and summer produced a new emigration of pilgrim warriors for the Holy Land." Bernard, one of the apostles of the crusades, applauds his own success in the depopulation of Europe. He affirms that cities and castles were emptied of their inhabitants, and computes that only one man was left behind for the consolation of seven widows. In view of all these historic statements, can we find no fulfillment of the prediction that they "*were to slay the third part of men?*"

Another striking feature characterizing the Turkish armies, was the multitude of their horsemen. In no other period of the world's history were such vast numbers of cavalry employed in war. It was not unusual for a Turkish leader to set forth on his campaigns, followed by two hundred thousand horsemen. The favorite expression of Gibbon in describing their armies is, "the myriads of Turkish horsemen." In the armies of the Greeks, the Romans, and the Goths, the infantry was always largely in excess of the cavalry; but with the Turks the very reverse was the case. The introduction of gunpowder in the fifteenth century, changed the method of warfare ; so that since the taking of Constantinople, no great military powers have been like the ancient Turks in the multitude of their horsemen. Remembering that they kept up these immense bodies of cavalry through a period of three centuries, is there no significance in the language of the revelator when he writes, "*The number of the army of the horsemen was two hundred thousand thousand,*" or as we would say, "myriads?" It is to be noted also, that this is the last time that such multitudes of earthly horsemen appear in the apocalyptic visions. This also corresponds, as I have just shown, with the facts of history. If a student of history was appointed to find out during what period cavalry was most exclusively used in warfare, and by what people, he would be compelled to say, "by the Turks, from A. D. 1050, to the fall of Constantinople, when gunpowder altered the mode of warfare."

A third characteristic of the Turkish horsemen, was

their apparel. The crusading knights and the soldiers of Europe wore armor; but these wild, fierce horsemen of the East disdained it, save at times a breastplate, and clad in bright garments of red and blue and yellow, they rushed to battle as to a feast. They are described by the historian as being "fierce as lions." Turkish valor and brutality became a proverb in the East and throughout Europe. Fire, pillage and extermination, or instant submission, were the only alternatives they offered.

The latter part of this period of warfare was marked by an invention, or discovery which has played a most important part ever since, in the world's history. It was the application of gunpowder to the deadly arts of war. "This mischievous discovery," says Gibbon, "over whose rapid progress, as compared with the laborious and slow advances of reason, science, and the arts of peace, a philosopher according to his temper, will laugh or weep," was soon communicated to the Turks, and by them used with deadly effect. They employed cannon at the siege of Constantinople; and it was amid the thunders of artillery, whose immense size still excites wonder and doubt, that the massive walls of the Imperial city fell; and the Turks rushed into the palaces of the Emperors, and transformed them into the courts and seraglios of their Sultans.

And now suppose that this historical period of 391 years, from the going forth of the Turkish power from Bagdad, to the taking of Constantinople, was spread out before us in one vast panorama; we saw the multitudes of horsemen in their gay apparel, starting on their errand of conquest; we marked their fierceness and valor; we saw the vast army of their victims from Europe; we beheld their mighty artillery, and witnessed for the first time the flames of fire and smoke belching forth from the mouths of their cannon;—suppose that we were required to describe all this in a few comprehensive, yet exact words, so that it might accurately be distinguished from all other movements in history, what better words could we select than those of St. John: "I saw a great host moving from the region of the Euphrates, destined to slay the third part of men. The number of the army was myriads, so great that I could not count them. I heard the number. I saw the horses and them that sat on them, having breastplates of fire, and of jacinth and brimstone; and the heads of the horses were as the heads of lions, and out of their mouths issued fire and smoke and brimstone."

I could, did our time permit, point out other points of correspondence, between the remaining part of the prophecy, and the history of the Turks. But surely there has been enough to establish the identification,

In conclusion, observe this: history tells us what a terror, plague, and judgment, the Turkish power has been to Christendom. But the Divine Word explains to us the design of this woe. It was God's judgment against idolatrous and superstitious Christianity. We read in verses twenty and twenty-one: "*And the rest of the men which were not killed by these plagues, yet repented not of the works of their hands, that they should not worship devils,* (i. e. demons or disembodied spirits,) *and idols of gold, and silver, and brass, and stone and of wood, which neither can see, nor hear, nor walk. Neither repented they of their murders, nor of their sorceries, nor of their fornications, nor of their thefts.*" In the former lecture, I quoted passages from history showing the lamentable condition of the Eastern Church during the time of the Saracen conquests. But instead of being restrained by judgments, the tide of idolatrous superstition increased. The fourteenth and fifteenth centuries were the dark ages of the Christian Church. The worship of saints, and relics, and images, became universal. As an illustration of the impious worship of the times, take the Psalter of St. Bonaventura, a cardinal, who took the Psalms of David, and wherever the word "Lord" or "God" occurred, substituted for it the name of the Virgin Mary. Lying miracles and pious frauds and relics abounded. A manual was issued under the pontificate of John XXII, in which every crime had its absolution, and every sin its forgiveness, for a fixed sum of money. Indulgences were sold publicly. Masses for the dead, the sale of ecclesiastical offices, and fees for licences to live in sin, brought in so great a revenue, that Pope Leo X. exclaimed, "how profitable this fable of Jesus Christ has been to us."

It was also the time of "murders," for sword and fire were freely used for the extinction of heresy. John Huss and his followers, the Waldenses, and the Albigenses were cruelly slaughtered in the name of Christianity. It is a sad and humiliating picture, which all historians present of Christendom in the middle ages; yet the opening of the sixteenth century found it under a cloud of accumulating and unrepented superstition. The facts of history confirm the statement of prophecy: "*neither repented they of their murders, nor of their sorceries, nor of their fornications, nor of their thefts.''*

How impressive is the lesson to be learned from these pages of history! God will establish His word to his believing children; and woe to those who, in the madness of their hearts, corrupt His truth, and resist His will. The perversion of Divine truth by an admixtion of human conceits and superstitions, is the last artifice of Satan in his assaults upon the church; it is one also, which he uses with deadly power. But the great Head of the church knew all of "his devices" from the beginning, and forewarned His people; and now that it has come to pass according to his word, we have no reason to "be offended" or cast down, as though Christianity itself were a failure. On the contrary, the events of history call to mind Christ's own sure testimony, "these things have I told you, that when the time shall come, ye may remember that I told you of them.

In this same revelation of "woes," we are told of those who were "sealed" or marked by God as his own. All through these judgments they were not forgotten. The hand that unloosed the powers of the Euphrates, and that dashed empires in pieces, "like a potter's vessel," was turned over these hidden ones to keep them in safety. Judgment brought them affliction, but caused them no harm or loss. By this "sealing," we are not to understand any outward mark upon the body, but that impress which regenerating grace makes on the inner man. The seal leaves an image of itself; so God in sealing His own, leaves His own image upon their souls. "The foundation of God standeth sure, having this seal; the Lord knoweth them that are His: and let every one that nameth the name of Christ depart from iniquity." Are you my hearers, "sealed" with this mark? Have you renounced the idolatries and ungodliness of a corrupt world, to serve the Lord in accordance with the testimony of His Word? Until you are thus made secure in Christ, the contemplation of the working of God's hand in history can fill you only with wonder and dread. How can you stand before Him, who breaks the power of a godless world and overwhelms with His judgments, the nations that despise His truth? Woes and terrors must track the steps of the impenitent and unbelieving, and sooner or later overtake them. There is no escape for us, until we have accepted Christ as a refuge, and are found in Him sealed by the renewing and sanctifying Spirit.

Lecture III.

The Decline of the Turkish Empire.

[Rev. 16: 12.]

AND the sixth angel poured out his vial upon the great river Euphrates; and the water thereof was dried up, that the way of the Kings of the East might be prepared.

IN the previous lecture, we found the prophecy recorded in Rev. 9: 13-19, fulfilled in the rise of the Turkish Empire, and in the woes which it inflicted upon Christendom. We identified the mighty army which came forth from "the great river Euphrates," with that military invasion, which swept like a desolating flood over the eastern part of the old Roman empire, burying both throne and altar in common ruin. We saw from the pages of history, that from the time the Turkish power became supreme in Bagdad, somewhere between A. D. 1056-62, until it enthroned itself in the palaces of the Christian emperors in Constantinople A. D. 1453, was a period of 391 years, and that this corresponds with the time assigned by prophecy, for its work of subversion. Then the work of overturning the eastern part of the apostate Christian empire was virtually done. The terrible threatenings which the apostle had uttered against the churches in case they did not repent, had come to pass. The "candlesticks" placed by apostolic hands, had been removed, and the land was left in terrible darkness, The "smoke" of Islamism which the revelator saw rising "out of the bottomless pit," enveloped the earth as with thick darkness.

Having thus seen the rise of this great military power, as pictured in prophecy, and verified in history, we are prepared to consider what prophecy has to say about its future. Passing on in the prophetic series, we again come "to the great river Euphrates," pictured to us as a river, which having overflowed its banks, has covered and desolated the surrounding region with its flood of waters. It is the very picture which Isaiah employed in his prophecy to represent the destructive conquests of the old Assyrian empire, spreading over the earth like a tide from the Euphrates. "Now therefore behold the Lord bringeth up upon them, the waters of the river, strong and many, even the king of Assyria and all his glory, And he shall come up over all his channels, and go over all his banks, and he shall pass through Judah, he shall overflow and go over: he shall reach even to the neck." Is. 8: 6, 8. Thus we have scriptural authority for designating the people and empire of a region by its chief river. In the Turkish invasion, how truly had the water of the "great river" been "brought up" against Christendom? It had overflowed, and gone over its banks, until its devastating torrents covered the land like a sea. In view of this, the voice of prophecy utters the history of the future in one brief yet most significant sentence—"*the great river Euphrates shall be dried up.*" Looking carefully at the prophecy, every candid mind will admit that the following statements are contained in it. 1. It points us to a power that has come from, and goes back to the region of the Euphrates, just as swollen waters come forth from, and go back to their native channels. 2. This power is to decline gradually. The picture of its decline is that of a river swollen by floods, drying up, until at last its channel is empty. 3. This power, until dried up, stands in the way of another movement, that of "*the Kings of the East.*" It lies across their way, like an unbridged and impassable stream; but its evaporation, removes the hindrance, and opens "the way." 4. This drying up is accomplished by divine judgments of various kinds, within the power itself. The vial which is poured out on the Euphrates, differs strikingly in its effects, from all the others. Its ingredients are just such as cause a wasting, or evaporation of all strength. It does not indicate that the power upon which it falls shall be cast down "with violence," like the mystic Babylon.

As to the time and place of this event in the prophetic series, this much may be said. The events described in the last lecture, occurred under the sounding of the sixth trumpet. Following this, is the seventh and last prophetic epoch, heralded by the sounding of the seventh trumpet. You will find upon examination, that this period corresponds with that predicted by the prophet Daniel, as the time when the Ancient of Days should come to judge the nations, and to give the kingdom to the Son of Man. It has been justly remarked, that "the sacred calendar, and great almanac of prophecy consists of the four kingdoms of Daniel, which are a prophetical chronology of times, measured by the succession of four principal kingdoms, from the beginning of the captivity of Israel, until the mystery of God should be finished." When this period is finished, the gospel of Christ shall be triumphant. It must be remembered that in making interpretations as to prophetic and historic periods, we must see that they accord with both Daniel and John, for the Word of God must not contradict itself. Both Daniel and John testify that this period, which one represents by the "coming of the Ancient of Days," (Dan. 7: 9-14.) and the other by the "seventh trumpet," is the last one in the divine dealings with great anti-christian and worldpowers, and that its issue shall be in this glorious consummation: "all the kingdoms of this world are become the kingdoms of our Lord, and of his Christ." Both, also, agree in representing it as a long one, in which judgment and mercy are mingled. To this era belong the judgments described by the "seven vials:" that is, the seven vials are poured forth while the seventh trumpet is sounding. But there is this peculiarity to be observed about the judgments represented by the vials. They are synchronous; that is, they are all poured forth at the same time, or at least nearly so.

We are expressly told that the trumpets sounded in their order; each one ceased, before the one to follow it began to sound. But the command to the seven angels to pour out their vials, is given to all at the same time. We are to understand by this that the judgment inflicted by one, was not necessarily exhausted, before another began. So that in searching history to find the realizations of the judgments represented by the vials, we must look especially to the localities on which they fell, rather than for the order of their coming.

Let us now turn to the pages of history, and it must be also, to the history of a locality occupied by the power which overflowed like a flood, from the region of the Euphrates, for it is there that the prophecy points. We have already identified this power with the Turkish Empire. When the sixth trumpet ceased its sounding, we found it enthroned in the ancient capital of the Roman world, the terror and plague of Christendom. Since that time no other power has come forth from the Euphrates, and the Turkish empire still remains. At the beginning of the eighteenth century, 640 years after Togrul had established his throne at Bagdad, the Turkish empire was still a formidable power in the world. Although shorn of nearly one half of its European possessions, it was abundantly able to defend itself. But before another century had gone by, the work of decay had begun. As though some invisible judgment had been poured out upon the empire, it was smitten with a blight which is destined to destroy it utterly. The period of its manifest decline began about A. D. 1800, and so rapid has been the process of the drying up of all its powers as a nation, that now it is but a shadow of its former greatness. For years past it has been known as the "sick man" of Europe; nor has any cure been found for its wasting consumption. It is a well known fact that Turkey, as a political power, exists only by sufferance. She has no inherent strength, no financial power, no resources as a nation to enable her to stand against her enemies.

Even as long ago as A. D. 1834, Lamartine in the French House of Deputies said: "The Ottoman empire is no empire at all. It is a misshapen agglomeration of different races without cohesion between them—with mingled interests, without a language, without laws, without religion, without unity of power. You see that the breath of life which animated it, namely religious fanaticism, is extinct; you see that its fatal and blinded administration has devoured the race of conquerers, and that Turkey is perishing for want of Turks." A late resident in Turkey after recounting her misfortunes, writes: "Her treasury exhausted, her trade and manufactures destroyed, her wonted revenues from the provinces and all her sources of wealth dried up, she sits an object of pitiable helplessness among the nations." So weak and contemptible has she become, that to-day with her successful armies in the field, she must carefully obey the commands of the powers that protect her, or forfeit her life. A writer and traveler long resident in the East, after speaking of the waste, ruin and decay within the Turkish empire, uses these significant words—"It is not too much to say that there is more of human life wasted, and less supplied, (in Turkey) than in any other country. We see every day, life going out in the fairest portion of Europe, and the human race threatened with extinction in a soil and climate capable of supporting the most abundant population."

Now observe what is peculiar about the decline of the Turkish power. It has been brought about by causes within itself. It is not by powers from without, hostile to it, that it has been destroyed. On the contrary, it has been singularly protected, and exempted from foreign wars by the jealousy of European powers. The battle of Navarino, and the Russian war of A. D. 1828, were indeed severe blows to the power of the Ottoman empire, but they were not the causes of its decline.

The causes are these. 1. Its government. Prophecy described it as the rule of "serpents." It was to be base, cruel and deadly. How literally this has been fulfilled, the dark annals of Turkish rule, or rather misrule tells us. There is nothing more terrible or oppressive in all history. It has been a government of weakness and wickedness combined, and under it the most glorious regions of the world, the lands of prophecy and of classic culture, the early homes of religion and of art, have been made desolate. Let us rejoice that it is near its end, and that this foul race of conquerers is doomed by the word of God, and the judgments of history to perish from the land it has ruined. A recent writer, whose history of the Saracen Conquests justly entitles him to be quoted as an authority, says—"The rule of the Turks is not government, it is the mere domination of a gang of robbers. If a burglar breaks into our house, we do not call it misgovernment; and the so called government of the Turks is simply an act of burglary prolonged for centuries." "Wherever" says Layard, "the Osmanli has placed his foot, he has bred fear and distrust. His visit has been one of oppression and rapine. The scarlet cap, and the well known garb of a Turkish irregular, are the signals for a grand panic."

Read the accounts of Turkish barbarities, of their robberies and oppressions, practiced upon their own subjects in these latter days, and you may have some faint conception of what their rule has been for ages; and you may understand, also, why under long centuries of oppression, the population of Turkey has decreased and become abject and base. Ever since the Crimean war, and in face of promised reforms, the testimony of the noblest man Christendom could send, would not stand in any Mahometan court of justice in the Turkish empire, against the vilest and most ignorant Moslem picked up from the gutter and hired for a piaster to testify in the case. The Mahometan law makes it impossible that the testimony of a Christian should be received as against that of a Moslem. No Christian, be he prince or patriarch, can be the equal of the basest Moslem; his life is spared only by sufferance. Cursed by such a government, we need not wonder that the Ottoman empire has had within itself terrible insurrections, and that it has been the author of its own weakness and wasting. Nor can this government be reformed. It is based on the Koran, which furnishes both civil and religious law for the Moslem. To change it, is to destroy the supremacy of the Turk.

2. Another cause of its decay is polygamy. This is one of the chief social curses of Asia, and like a deadly blight, it has turned some of the fairest portions of the East into a desert. Destroying the sacredness of the family relation as instituted by God, it becomes a source of disorder and destruction in society. Some have claimed that Mahomet, by limiting the number of wives to four, had in some measure reformed polygamy. By no means. We cannot reform that which is essentially wrong. The difference between taking one wife and two,

is immeasurably great; but the difference between two and two thousand is comparatively nothing. The first is a difference of principle; the second, only of expense. The social life of the Turk, which finds its nourishment in the harem, is on this account low and base. Said an intelligent man, one who had resided twenty-five years in Syria—"the Turks are the vilest people under the sun. Their beastiality would disgrace Sodom."

3. The third cause of their decay is their religion. It was from the first a wild, fierce fanaticism, and so it is doomed to expire. At the outstart, its great principle of fatalism had a wonderful power in animating its followers; but its last effects are ruinous in the extreme. When the fever of enthusiasm excited by it is over, this same doctrine leads to opposite results, and begets listlessness and inactivity. "Nothing," says Freeman, "is so energetic as a Mahometan nation in its youth; nothing is so utterly feeble as a Mahometan nation in its old age." As the Koran is the chief authority both in religious and civil matters, reform is an impossibility in the Turkish empire. Reform is its destruction: religion or the church, the family, and the government, are the three vital organs of society; and when these are all bad, and incurably so, we can only wait for the time of the dissolution. There is no cure. In view of all these causes which have brought down this mighty empire, once the terror of Europe, to its present exhausted and decrepit condition, can we doubt the accuracy of the prophecy, uttered nine hundred years before this empire appeared in history;—"*The water of the Euphrates was dried up:*" do we not find within the empire itself, the judgment that has wasted its power, and

evaporated all its strength? The "waters of the Euphrates," once so broad, are now but as a little rill, and it too, shall soon disappear. It is a well known fact that Turkey to-day, owes its outward existence, simply to the jealousy of European powers; and now a new danger threatens to obliterate it entirely from the map of Europe. There is no power in Turkey to hinder the troops of the Czar from reaching the gates of Constantinople, should they once start on their march. There might be a temporary flaming forth of the old religious fanaticism, and the famous war-cry of "Allah" be heard along the excited ranks of the Turks; but it will only be a feeble echo of the shout that once rolled like the noise of the sea, from the hosts of Othman, or Mahomet II. The great question in Europe to-day, is not the conquest of Turkey, but how to get rid of the dead body of an old empire, and administer on its effects to the satisfaction of all parties.

Thus far we have been able to place prophecy and history side by side, and to confirm the revelations of the one, by the facts of the other. But we have come to a period in which history ends. Men are busy writing it day by day, and we look eagerly to see what tomorrow will bring. But the prophecy does not stop; it runs on with confident utterances, saying, *"and the water thereof was dried up, that the way of the Kings of the East might be prepared."*

The next act in the great drama, is the "preparation of the way." Something is to transpire, which shall not only remove the curse of Mahometan rule from the Euphrates to the Nile, but it will also open up the way for another glorious event—a new rule, a new kingdom—that of "*Kings of the East.*" Even now God's engineers are preparing for work on this new way, and it may be that cannon and the sword, and the whirlwind of battle, shall be among the divinely appointed agencies in opening it up. Diplomacy and national jealousy may delay the result for a time, but it shall surely come in God's appointed hour, for the mouth of the Lord has spoken it. Three great powers, Austria, France, and England, are each bound by solemn and separate treaties to declare war on any state, and especially Russia, should it invade Turkish soil; yet, in the providence of God, those treaties have been made nullities! France will not uphold them, Austria cannot, and public sentiment in England will not suffer a war to keep the miserable Moslem rule in power. National ambition cannot stand supreme over the interests of humanity. The sentiment of the age, the demands of Christianity, and the pleadings of outraged and oppressed humanity, demand that this nation of usurpers and serpent-rulers shall be driven out of Europe, and back to their native deserts in Asia. All cry for the new rule,—"the Kings of the East." There is only one power in Christendom that sympathises with the Turk, and this is exactly in accordance with the intimations of prophecy. It is that of the Pontiff in the Vatican. I will read the proof of this from the chief catholic organ in the world: "Russia," it says "is the most inveterate and malignant enemy of the Church of God, of all the sovereignties now standing on the globe. The dominion of the Turk, bad as it is, is more advantageous to catholic interests, both in Europe and Asia, than is the dominion of the Czar." Prophecy you will observe.

is silent as to the manner of "this preparation of the way." It is not impossible that the arms of contending European states should clash on the plains of Turkey. But certainly, prophecy does not specify in this connection any violent or notable war. That is to come at a later date. Nor is the "time," during which the preparation of the way shall extend, given; but certain it is, that events indicate speedy and great changes, and we can live in daily and confident expectation of their coming to pass.

We cannot set times and dates for the future, when God has not revealed them; but in view of the rapid developments of the present, it is not presumption to say that there is some one now alive, who shall before his earthly career ends, look upon a new map of the world, in which he will search in vain for the empire of the Turks.

But, the Mahometan power removed, what next? What power will take its place? What is the nature of that strife which makes it necessary for Turkish rule to be out of the way? When Gibbon closed his thrilling history of the crusades, he summed up in a few words the story of its carnage and desolations, described the departure of the feeble remnants of the mighty hosts of Christendom from the shores of Palestine, and then added as a last touch, these words:—"and a mournful and solitary silence prevailed along the coast, which had so long resounded with the WORLD'S DEBATE." That debate was whether Christianity or Islamism should rule in Syria. But it was not closed then. The "World's Debate" broke out again in war. Strange to say, the Crimean war grew out of the question of the keys of a church in Jerusalem, just as the crusades grew out of the oppression of Christians in their worship, in the same place. To-day, the impending conflict is of the same character. It may not be known to all, but the official appeal of the Sultan's government calls upon his faithful subjects to enlist in "the Holy war against the Infidel " The firman telegraphed through the empire. calling for subscriptions to the war fund, entitles it, "Religious War Aid Fund." This is its aspect on the Turkish side. On the other, it is proclaimed to be a movement in behalf of oppressed Christians. If the crescent and the cross meet, who can doubt the issue? But it is not by the sword, that the true gospel triumphs. Sword and battle may prepare the way; they are God's pioneers to remove barriers, and take away hindrances, but the gospel is something essentially different in its workings.

Imagine the oppression of Turkish rule taken off the region that it now occupies, the crescent supplanted by the cross on the dome of St. Sophia, and the mosque of Omar—what wonderful and beneficient changes must follow? A land, by nature one of the richest and most fertile on the earth, a land which draws its pilgrims from every quarter of the earth, to visit the ruins of its former greatness, would soon be redeemed and made to bloom like a garden. "The Kings of the East," the new power that is to take the place of the old, who are they? This is the question the future is to answer. Prophecy gives us hints concerning it, which we will consider on a future occasion. I can only say now, it is not Russia. The latter may be God's chosen pioneer to open the way for the "Kings of the East," but it is not the power destined to rule over the land of promise.

And now, if the interpretation I have given you is true, we are able to know our place in the course of time. The seventh trumpet is sounding, and its stirring notes of mingled warning and mercy are carried on the air. Great voices in heaven, the voices of those who watch the struggles of the Church on earth, are crying in anticipation,—"the kingdoms of this world are become the kingdoms of our Lord and of his Christ, and he shall reign forever and ever." Surely it is something to be thankful for, that our lot has been cast in so glorious an era, one so full of hope and mighty incentives to labor for Christ. The power of Christ is daily becoming more manifest in the world, and his enemies are more bitter and outspoken. The hour also, seems to be at hand, when he shall make a still more glorious revelation of his power. Who among you can rejoice in the triumphs of his cross, and look with eager hope for the day of his appearing?

Again, if it be true that we are now on the eve of the fulfillment of the prophecy that declared the drying up of the Euphratean waters, we know that it is time for us to be specially on our guard; for this is the message which the Spirit utters; "Behold, I come as a thief. Blessed is he that watcheth and keepeth his garments, lest he walk naked, and they see his shame."

Lecture IV.

The Kings of the East.

[Rev. 16:12.]

AND the water therof was dried up, that the way of the Kings of the East might be prepared.

THE judgment symbolized by the pouring out of the sixth vial upon the great river Euphrates, is to find its fulfillment in the gradual decline of the Turkish Empire. But the same prophecy declares that this event shall be followed by another—a preparation for a new rule—that of "the Kings of the East." The manner or method of this preparation is not described, nor is the time of its duration given; nor is there any description of the rule of the Kings of the East. It is an event sure to come, but which can be recognized with certainty only when it does come to pass. This much, however, is fairly inferable from the prophecy: First, it is an advanced step toward the Kingdom of Christ; it is to be regarded as a blessing, and not as a "woe" or judgment, like the Ottoman power. Second, it is reasonable to say that this power called "the Kings of the East," is one already in existence at the time when the revelator is writing. You will observe that when any of the prophets, and especially St. John, speaks of a new power appearing for the first time in history, he describes its origin. Thus he describes the Saracen power as "locusts" born out of the "smoke." The Turkish power is described as "horsemen" coming forth from the Euphrates. But here he alludes to the Kings of the East as already existing, for the "great river Euphrates," until dried up, was an obstacle in their path. His language also fairly implies that this power already existing, is waiting its opportunity in time to take its rightful and God-appointed place. This opportunity is to come after the downfall of the Turkish Empire. So much we can fairly gather from the prophecy itself.

In attempting to reach some conclusions as to the nature of this predicted preparation and power, I wish to repeat what I said in a previous discourse—that, while the prophecy is sure, my application of it, or any man's application of it, to events yet future, may be erroneous. In interpreting unfulfilled prophecy, the only safe rule is to keep in view the way in which prophecy has already passed into history. God's method of working in nature does not change; the past is a type of the future; so also is it in His providential government of the world. There is indeed an order of advancement, a forward and upward march to the appointed end; but through all, run the same principles and methods which have been illustrated in the history of the past and present. Again, we must interpret prophecy by prophecy. That which is to come, is related to that which is past. There is a unity in prophecy as there is in history; one great design runs through both. So it often happens that some part of a prophecy, dark and puzzling by itself, becomes luminous and intelligible when fitted to its place among the other parts that go to make up the whole design. Keeping these principles in view, let us attempt the solution of the question before us.

One class of interpreters have seen in this declaration, *"And the water thereof was dried up, that the way of the Kings of the East might be prepared,"* nothing more than a declaration in general, that the downfall of the Turkish Empire would begin a new era for the kingdoms of Asia, by opening up their way for the enjoyment of a higher civilization, and for the possession of the Gospel. Those old kingdoms and dynasties, so long cursed with oppression, ignorance, and superstition, would feel the power of a new life among them, consequent upon the introduction of Christian civilization. The removal of the Turkish power would prepare the way for the evangelization of the kingdoms of the East.

All this is undoubtedly true. The Turkish rule, the embodiment of Islamism, has been a curse to Asia as well as a plague to Europe. It has spread like a flood over the great highway of the world's trade and commerce, and for 800 years made it impassable. Europe had to seek Asia by the Cape of Good Hope. The social life and the government established by Mahometans have been a "hindrance" to the nations of the East; Mahometanism more than heathenism, has been an obstacle to the spread of the Gospel. It is death for any of its adherents to embrace Christianity. All of the essential conditions of its rule are hostile to the Gospel, for the latter does not thrive in an atmosphere of tyranny and immorality. Unquestionably, the removal of the Turkish rule would be a blessing to civilization, to humanity and to religion. It would open the old channel of trade and commerce to the heart of Asia, so long blocked up, and along this highway would go the influences that would renew the lands of the East. The manhood of oppressed Christians would be developed, the blessings of a just rule and stable laws be brought to them, education would displace ignorance and superstition, and thus, all working together, would prepare the way for the triumph of Christianity. It is not unreasonable to suppose that the utter downfall of the Turkish Empire would mark the beginning of new and better days for Asia. In this the interpreter of prophecy, the student of history, and the statesman, all agree.

But is this all the prophecy means? If so, it tells nothing new, beyond what is affirmed in general terms in scores of other places in the Word of God. The Gospel proclaims itself to be a world-conquering religion. It predicts its own triumph, and in sublime confidence asserts that all convulsions and tumults, all overturning of empires and uprisings of new ones, are directly in its interest. It asserts, again and again, that it is a light for all lands, and that all that hinders it shall be cast down. In view of these general predictions, certainly it would not require any great gift of the spirit of prophecy to affirm, that the overturning of the Turkish Empire would be in the interests of Christianity, and would prove a great blessing to the people of the East; but if the spirit of prophecy be necessary to affirm this result, then the mantle of the prophets must rest upon the vast majority of our editors and public men, for they are vehemenently affirming the same declaration. The view of the interpreters just alluded to, is doubtless true in general, but it does not seem to me to meet all the demands of the case.

1. Naturally, with the rule of the Turks destroyed, we think of the land over which it extended—and, the more especially, as it happens to be the land of prophecy, in which the predictions of this Word center.

If you will look at a modern map, you will find that the Turkish rule extends over that region of country lying between the river Euphrates and the Nile. It is the very region which God gave, by solemn covenant, to Abraham and his sons, to be theirs forever.

We read in Genesis, 15: 18: In the same day the Lord made a covenant with Abram, saying: "Unto thy seed have I given this land, from the river of Egypt. unto the great river, the river Euphrates." Again, in repeating the covenant, Jehovah said: "I will give unto thee and to thy seed after thee, the land wherein thou art a stranger, all the land of Canaan for an everlasting possession; and I will be their God." Genesis 17: 8.

This is the land upon which the "waters" of the river Euphrates" have overflowed, and from which they are to be "dried up." Remembering that prophecy reveals to us God's plans and purposes for the future, what people should we expect to eventually occupy this land, if not those to whom He gave it for an everlasting possession? God appoints the lot of nations as well as of men. It is not by accident that one is planted here, and another there. Suppose the Spaniard instead of the Puritan, had settled upon the shores of New England, how different would the history of this country have been: or, had the Latin instead of the Saxon races found their homes and dominion in the north of Europe, the history of its civilization would have been changed.

For reasons of the highest importance in the development of His own plans for the redemption of man, God assigned a chosen land to the "Chosen People." The land was of His choice, and the title deed to it is invested, while time shall last, in the descendants of Abraham. The Christian will recognize the right of the Jew to his ancestral lands; and even among the Mahometans there is a traditional saying, "that they do not own the Holy Land, but only hold it until God's purpose shall be fulfilled." The land or locality now held under Moslem rule, leads us to think of the Jews as its rightful kings or rulers, because it belongs to them by a divine charter that has never been repealed. John wrote the Revelation twenty years after the destruction of Jerusalem and the dispersion of the Jews from the Holy Land—and his language tried by a fair and honest interpretation, certainly means that the power which is to come in after the removal of the Turkish rule, is a rightful one, now withheld or restrained by certain obstacles.

2. Observe another hint or intimation which is given in the language of the prophecy: the phrase, "Kings of the East" or "from the rising of the sun," evidently designates something else than ordinary kingdoms and rulers, for we can see by what follows in the fourteenth verse, that they stand separate and distinct from "the kings of the earth and of the whole world."

Remember that we are to interpret this language in the light of Old Testament distinctions and usage. Of what other people save of the Jews, can it be affirmed that God has chosen them from among all the families of the earth to be a nation of "kings and priests unto Him?" Is it not true that, in distinction from "the kings of the earth and of the whole world," he has chosen them for a peculiar mission, and to be the witnesses alike of his mercy and his wrath through the ages?

3. As the revelator draws all his imagery from the Old Testament, or in accordance with its usages, the allusion in this prophecy is evidently to Isaiah 44; 27—"Thus saith the Lord thy Redeemer—that saith to the deep, be dry: and I will dry up thy rivers." This, as you will see, refers to the restoration of the Jews from the Babylonian captivity. One hundred and fifty years before that event came to pass, Isaiah prophesied as to the manner in which it was to be done. He names not only the king whom God would raise up to accomplish it, but he describes the particular act on which, as on a pivot, the whole fortunes of war and empire turned. Babylon, the mighty capital of the Babylonian empire, which with iron hand held the Jews in bondage, was pronounced impregnable. So when Cyrus, the Persian, approached the city with his army, the proud descendants of Nebuchadnezzar simply closed the gates of the city, and behind the towering and massive walls continued their feasts, careless of danger. The river Euphrates ran through the city, and Cyrus conceived the plan, as Heroditus tells us, of diverting the river from its course, and then assaulting the city through its dried-up channels. This he accomplished, and thus in the manner described by Isaiah, the great Babylon-

ian empire was overturned, and a way opened for the return of the Jews. On this pivotal point, on which everything turns for the moment, the eyes of the prophet rest. Isaiah writes, "God saith I will dry up thy rivers." Jeremiah writes, a "sword is upon the inhabitants of Babylon, a drought is upon her waters, and they shall be dried up. I will dry up her sea and make her springs dry." We say, "that history repeats itself," that is, each nation is continually finding in its history circumstances corresponding essentially with former events, only they are higher up as it were in an ascending spiral.

So prophecy, which is the foreshadowing of history, finds likenesses, and declares them by using the imagery which described one set of events already fulfilled, to set forth another of the same general character still in the future.

How significant then is the allusion of St. John to the former deliverance from the Babylonian captivity! The people whose deliverance then turned upon the drying up of the Euphrates, were the Jews, whom Babylonish power prevented from returning to their own land. Again, he tells us, the water of the Euphrates is to "be dried up"—that is, a power overcome, that the way may be prepared for a people kept back by it from their inheritance.

Starting with these points or suggestions drawn from the passage before us, let us turn to the general scope of prophecy as it treats of the future of the Jews, and see if any light will shine upon this "dark saying."

If John is a true prophet, he must be in harmony with Isaiah, and Jeremiah, and Daniel, and Zechariah.

If he is here speaking of the Jews, what he says must correspond with what the prophets preceding him have testified concerning the same people. You are familiar with the predictions by which it was disclosed to Abraham, that his seed should inherit Canaan for an everlasting possession. You know also, that after a period of over 400 years spent in bondage, the prediction was realized. The seed of Abraham, preserved as by a miracle, came in possession of the promised land; but when led into it, the Divine Voice announced a series of judgments that should fall upon them, in case they were false to Jehovah. These are distinctly recorded in the twenty-sixth chapter of the book of Leviticus. If you will carefully examine that chapter, you will find that it is an exact forecasting, in their order, of the terrible judgments which were to come, and which have come upon Israel. The last in the series is described as the most severe and destructive. It is a description of the judgment which began at the destruction of Jerusalem. "I will destroy your high places; I will make your cities waste and bring your sanctuaries unto destruction; and I will bring the land into desolation, and your enemies which dwell therein shall be astonished at it. I will scatter you among the heathen, and your land shall be desolate, and your cities waste; and they that are left of you shall pine away in their iniquity in your enemies' lands, and also in the iniquities of their fathers shall they pine away with them." "I will sift the house of Israel among the nations like as corn is sifted in a sieve, yet shall not the least grain fall upon the earth." Amos 9: 9. "I will deliver them to be removed into all the kingdoms of the earth for their hurt, to be a reproach and a proverb, a taunt, and curse in all places whither I shall drive them." Jer. 24 : 9, 10. Such are a few of the many predictions concerning their last dispersion among the Gentiles. And what has history to say concerning them? "The land of Judea is indeed a desolation; its cities are in ruins, its fields naked and bare, so that the plains, which were once the granaries of the world, do not yield enough of corn to supply the scanty population abiding there." Jerusalem is "trodden down of the Gentiles," according to the prediction of Jesus Christ. The place of the sanctuary is profaned by the mosque and worship of the false prophet. Taken away from the land of his fathers, the Jew has indeed been "sifted" like corn among the nations. We find him in all lands, north, south, east, and west. He is among all people, yet separated and distinct from all. His national characteristics are as clearly manifest now, as in the days of Solomon. The sons of Abraham on the banks of the Mississippi are still marked by the features of their illustrious sire, and many a Jewish maiden represents the fair counterpart of the beauteous Rebecca; and still, perhaps, some son of Jacob weeps for joy as he kisses her and discovers the loving kinship between them. The Jew is the miracle of history. By all the laws that govern other tribes and races, he ought to have been absorbed and lost among the nations, as the waters of a smaller stream are lost in the current of a mighty river. But instead of this, he has survived the races of his conquerers and oppressors. Egypt and her Pharaohs, the Babylonians, the Persians, the Grecians, and the Romans—all these are dead and buried in their graves beyond the hope of resurrection. But the Jew still lives, as when Pharaoh oppressed him; or when he sung his songs by the rivers of Babylon in sad exile, or when the Romans carried him away to wander for ages among the Gentiles. Who can adequately describe their sorrows, or picture the hardships of their lot! Everywhere they have been pursued, tormented, persecuted and slaughtered. Literally their name has been a taunt, and an epithet of scorn and derision. Romans and Christians slaughtered them, or drove them as fugitives to the uttermost parts of the earth, until, in the time of Constantine, there were only 500 of them left in Palestine. The Mahometans slew them by thousands. The history of the Crusades is stained with the accounts of the murders of this hapless people, in the cities and towns of Europe. Gibbon tells us, in touching lines, of the thousands of helpless Jews who fell as victims to the fanatical rage of the christian Crusaders. Sir Walter Scott, in describing the sufferings of this people, writes: "Except, perhaps, the flying-fish, there was no race existing on the earth, in the air, or in the water, who were the objects of such an unremitting, general and relentless persecution as the Jews of this period. Upon the slightest and most unreasonable pretences, as well as upon accusations the most absurd and groundless, their persons and their property were exposed to every turn of popular fury; for Norman, Saxon, Dane and Briton, however adverse the races were to each other, contended which should look with the greatest detestation upon a people whom it was accounted a point of religion to hate, to revile, to despise, to plunder and to persecute."

Thus, for eighteen centuries, have the Jews been despoiled and persecuted. They have been a proverb, a hissing and a by-word, as prophecy proclaimed more than three thousand years ago. Yet 10,000,000 of them remain. Why are they so strangely presevered?

In this same connection you will find a prediction concerning Jerusalem. It was written by the prophet Zechariah after the Babylonian captivity. "Behold, I will make Jerusalem a cup of trembling unto all the people round about. And in that day will I make a burdensome stone for all people; all that burden Jerusalem themselves with it shall be cut in pieces, though all the people of the earth be gathered together against it." Zech. 12: 2-3. What is the testimony of history with reference to this? According to the word of our Lord, Jerusalem has been "trodden down of the Gentiles" for eighteen centuries; but during all that time it has been a plague and a burden to those who held it. The Romans found it a burden. It cost the Saracens untold treasure and blood to keep it, and finally, they were destroyed. The Crusaders held it for a century, but found it a burdensome stone, greater than Europe could carry. The Turks have held it, and have already had three wasting wars in its behalf. Jerusalem in ruins has been a question of debate,—a perpetual strife and burden to the nations.

And now let us take a step farther. On the same page of prophecy, written by the same pen, we find declarations affirming the restoration of Jerusalem, and of the chosen people to the inheritance of their fathers. Let us hear some of these predictions: "I will bring them again also out of the land of Egypt, and gather them out of Assyria; and I will bring them into the land of Gilead and Lebanon." Zech. 10: 10. This was written after the Babylonian captivity, so it cannot refer to the return at that time. Jesus Christ said: "And they shall fall by the edge of the sword. Jerusalem shall be trodden down of the Gentiles until the times of the Gentiles be fulfilled." Luke 21: 24. Does not this imply that there is a time of restoration?

Paul writes: "For I would not, brethren, that ye should be ignorant of this mystery (that is, the judgment which has fallen upon the Jews,) lest ye should be wise in your own conceits, that blindness in part is happened to Israel until the fullness of the Gentiles be come in." The universal testimony of the prophets is this: "I will bring them again into the land that I gave unto their fathers. Behold, I will send for many fishers saith the Lord, and they shall fish them; and after will I send for many hunters, and they shall hunt them from every mountain and from every hill, and out of the holes of the rocks."

The prophet Zechariah writing after the Babylonish captivity, records this prediction concerning the chosen people: "And they shall be as mighty men which tread down their enemies in the mire of the streets in the battle: and they shall fight because the Lord is with them, and the riders on horses shall be confounded." (One might fancy that there is an allusion here to those whom St. John describes as "the great army of horsemen.") "And I will strengthen the house of Judah, and I will save the house of Joseph, and I will bring them again to place them; for I have mercy upon them; and they shall be as though I had not cast them off; for I am the Lord their God and will hear them. And they of Ephraim shall be like a mighty man, and their heart shall rejoice as through wine; yea their children shall see it, and be glad; their heart shall rejoice in the Lord. I will hiss for them and gather them; for I have redeemed them: and they shall increase as they have increased. And I will sow them among the people; and they shall remember me in far countries: and they shall live with their children and turn again. I will bring them again also out of the land of Egypt, and gather them out of Assyria; (that is, like as He had formerly delivered them from their Egyptian and Assyrian captivity, so would He again restore them,) and I will bring them into the land of Gilead and Lebanon; and place shall not be found for them. And he shall pass through the sea with affliction, and shall smite the waves in the sea;—(God shall prepare the way for their return on the one side, as He did when He divided the Red Sea, for the escape of Israel,)—and all the deeps of the river shall dry up, (the allusion here is to the waters of the Euphrates, the representation of Assyria:) and the pride of Assyria shall be brought down, and the sceptre of Egypt shall depart away. And I will strengthen them in the Lord; and they shall walk up and down in his name, saith the Lord." Zech. 10: 5-12.

A careful examination of the prophecies concerning the future of the Jews will show that their return from Babylonian captivity, and the circumstances attending it, are used as a type of their return from their last captivity and dispersion among the Gentiles. For example, Isaiah writes; "thus saith the Lord thy Redeemer, that confirmeth the word of his servant, and performeth the counsel of his messengers; that saith to Jerusalem, Thou shalt be inhabited; and to the cities of Judah, Ye shall be built; and I will raise up the decayed places thereof; that saith to the deep, Be dry; and I will dry up thy rivers." (Is. 44: 26, 27.) Here the reference is primarily to the return from Babylon; but we have only to read on in the next chapter to find that he uses it as the type of a still more glorious restoration in the future. We find then, that Isaiah and Zechariah declare that the drying up of the waters of the river Euphrates shall prepare a highway for the return of Israel to their own land; and here in the Revelation, St. John declares that the same event will prepare the way for the Kings of the East.

If we let prophecy interpret prophecy, what shall we say other than this,—that the Kings of the East are that peculiar people whom God has from the ages and centuries past, appointed to rule in the regions between the river of Egypt and the great river Euphrates.

We have found the first part of these prophecies literally fulfilled; by what right, then, can we give a spiritual interpretation to that which remains to be fulfilled, and remove it from the realms of history to that of mystical and spiritual fulfillment? The only sensible and safe rule is to say, that just as part of the prophecy, that which relates to the dispersion and captivity of the Jews, has been translated into history, in like manner what remains shall be fulfilled, that is,— the dispersion was a literal one, so shall the restoration be. The Jew shall again dwell in peace in the land of his fathers, for the mouth of his God hath spoken it.

In view of all this, you can, my hearers, decide for yourselves as to the identity of the Kings of the East. But as it seems to me, God in his providence is now preparing the way for the calling back of his ancient people to their ancestral homes. And this, as I propose to show you in the next lecture, is one of the predicted steps toward the coming end.

Suffer me in conclusion, to draw a practical lesson from this. I have been speaking to you of the fate of the Jews, the people upon whom God in a special manner poured out his mercy, and to whom he sent the promised Redeemer. You know the secret of the judgment that has sent them forth as homeless wanderers on the face of the earth. They meet you every day to remind you how mercy outraged and despised, turns into wrath. You are free to pass judgment upon them, and to say that their terrible sentence is just. But who art thou, O man! that judgest another, when thou art in the same condemnation? Jesus Christ, the Lord, has stood at the door of your heart, seeking an entrance, but you would not prepare the way. You said in your unbelief, "I will not have this man to reign over me. Depart, thou Christ, I know thee not." Wherein is the unbelief of a Jew more criminal than that of you Gentiles, who have been taught from your youth the truth as it is in Jesus? Beware, lest often rejected, He turn away and leave you to your fate. There is no judgment so terrible as outraged and despised mercy.

Lecture V.

Steps Toward the End.

[Rev. 10: 7. 11: 14-15.]

BUT in the days of the voice of the seventh angel, when he shall begin to sound, the mystery of God should be finished, as he hath declared to his servants, the prophets.

The second woe is past; and behold, the third woe cometh quickly. And the seventh angel sounded; and there were great voices in heaven, saying, The kingdoms of this world are become the kingdoms of our Lord, and of his Christ; and he shall reign forever and ever.

IN the opening lecture in this series, prophecy was compared to a chart placed in the hands of voyagers sailing for the first time across the sea, to a new world. The chart is infallible, and on it are marked the rocks, and headlands, and lighthouses, by which the course to be sailed, lies. As far as the voyagers have actually gone on their journey, they have been able to verify the accuracy of the chart. It has brought them comfort and satisfaction, inasmuch as they are fully convinced that they are sailing under the direction of one who knows the way, and so is able to bring them to the desired haven. But if the chart is complete, they can also anticipate the time of their arrival, and say from what is revealed to them, "we are far off," or "we are near the end." At least, knowing what is past, they may say, "such and such objects must first appear to us in their proper order, before we reach the shore.

Can we say the same after studying that wonderful map of the future, drawn by the hands of prophets and apostles inspired by God? In so far as prophecy has been fulfilled we are able, at least in some measure, to verify it with the testimony of history. But with regard to that which is manifestly unfulfilled as yet, can we form any well founded conjectures from it, as to how far we are from the end? An end there is,—an era when the conflicts and judgments of time shall cease. The word of God in language that cannot be misunderstood, proclaims the final triumph of Jesus Christ, and His glorious reign in peace and righteousness. Our absent Lord is coming a second time, in glory instead of humiliation. The plain positive language of Scripture is—"This same Jesus which is taken up from you into heaven, shall so come in like manner as ye have seen Him go into heaven." Acts 1: 11.

But how soon? May He come to-morrow; or do events, as yet unfulfilled concerning His kingdom, place that "second coming" in the remote future? There are those who confidently say,—"the end is at hand." Nothing hinders the coming of that august day when the Lord shall appear in the clouds, and as with the voice of an archangel, and the trump of God, wake the dead that sleep in Jesus; and translate those who are alive and believe in Him, to meet Him in the air. They tell us that faith is weak, and love cold; that corruption abounds; that the church is powerless, and society, diseased to the core, is ready for dissolution. All these are to them the signs of the coming end.

It is curious to observe that since the time of the apostles, there has always been a class of men who were looking for the end of the world in their days. They have expected that when they left the world, the great drama of God's providence would come to an end, and that dissolving nature would form part of their own obsequies. But they have died, and ages have gone; the sun still shines, the mystery of human life is continued, and the end is not yet. Jesus Christ discoursing on this very subject, warned his disciples against hurried anticipations of the end, saying, "see that ye be not troubled; for all these things must come to pass; but the end is not yet." Men are always disposed to hasten the fulfillment of God's purposes, and to confound the beginning with the end. They forget the slow patient method of God's working, and the ages of delay, as measured by mortals, which have always characterized the ripening of his purposes. Perhaps our first impressions upon reading prophecy, unconsciously to ourselves, awaken anticipations of haste which the facts, if we only considered them, would not justify. When we read history where the events of a century are recorded on a few pages, read in a moment of time, it seems as if battle followed on the heels of battle, and that mankind did nothing but fight. We are oblivious of the fact that long years intervened between the recorded events.

So with prophecy, which is only history written beforehand. It reads as if all things were in perpetual commotion. One thunder peal has not died away until the next breaks on our ears. Trumpet sounds after trumpet, and the wondrous panorama brings events before us in such rapid succession, that we lose all sense of time, and look for the next moment to bring the final crash. To deliver ourselves from this feeling of panic and alarm with which many read prophecy, we must remember that it is the forecasting of centuries and ages of time.

In the opposite extreme are those who have deferred the end to so remote a period, that it has no practical effect upon their hopes and aspirations. They stand practically among the scoffers of the last days, saying, "Where is the promise of his coming? for since the fathers fell asleep, all things continue as they were from the beginning of the creation." Whether it is worse to live under a delusion as to the time of the end, or in forgetfulness of it, I will not attempt to decide. But let us for our own profit, carefully consider the testimony of God's word.

You will remember that the woes symbolized by the "locusts," and the "horsemen from the Euphrates," which we identified with the Saracens, and the Turkish power, occured under the soundings of the fifth and sixth trumpets. If this identification be correct, we are now in the period of time measured by the sounding of the seventh trumpet, or as the same period is marked by Daniel, in the time when the Ancient of Days is executing judgment. Dan. 7: 9. In this opinion all writers of any authority agree. The Revelation of St. John proclaims this period to be the last one of judgment and conflict with anti-christian and world-powers. We read in Rev. 10: 5-7. "And the angel which I saw stand upon the sea and the earth lifted up his hand to heaven, and sware by Him that liveth for ever and ever, that there should be time no longer," (Greek—"that the time shall be no more") *but in the days of the voice of the seventh angel, when he shall begin to sound, the mystery of God should be finished, as he hath declared to his servants the prophets.*"

Observe what is affirmed by this passage. It is not that the end of the world is to follow upon the close of the era represented by the seventh trumpet. Some have been led into a strange misinterpretation of the statement of the revelator, by the clause in our English version reading, "that there should be time no longer." They have supposed it was a declaration, that time in the abstract should cease to be, or in other words, that the great end of human history was now reached, and the drama of the present world was to close forever. But the original shows this to be a mistake. It is literally, "that the time should be no longer," that is, as explained in the next verse, the time of "the mystery of God," when the thunders of His judgments were sounding against reigning iniquity, apostacy and corruption. This period of conflict and judgment is to be continued until the pouring out of the seventh vial, the last one under the seventh trumpet, is completed. Then "the judgment shall no longer be;" the period of judgment is at an end. All this accords with the subsequent statement in the Revelation. When the seventh vial is poured out, there are "thunderings," but never after it.

Then, the mystery of God is finished. The rebellious and hostile powers are subdued and broken, and the way prepared for the establishment of the Messianic era, the glad millennium, the glorious reign of Christ, in which shall be fulfilled the joyous cry, *"the kingdoms of the world are become the kingdoms of our Lord and of His Christ."* In this testimony all the prophets agree. The language of Daniel (7: 14) coincides perfectly with that of St. John. After describing the period of judgment, he says, "Behold, one like the Son of Man; and there was given Him dominion, and glory, and a kingdom, that all people, nations, and languages, should serve Him: His dominon is an everlasting dominion, that shall not pass away." Isaiah, from his watchtower, seeing the same period in the future, cries, "they shall not hurt nor destroy in all my holy mountain; for the earth shall be full of the knowledge of the Lord, as the waters cover the sea." Is. 11: 9. In describing the Messiah's reign, the Psalmist says, "In His days shall the righteous flourish; and abundance of peace so long as the moon endureth. He shall have dominion also, from sea to sea, and from the river unto the ends of the earth. They that dwell in the wilderness, shall lick the dust. All nations shall call Him blessed." Ps. 72. Zechariah, writes, "And the Lord shall be king over all the earth; in that day there shall be one Lord and His name one." Zech. 14: 9. There are many such testimonies uttered by the prophets, all showing that they believed in a coming time when the powers of a hostile world would be utterly overthrown, and their discomfiture followed by a long and happy reign of gospel truth. All interpreters of prophecy, nay, all who believe in the Scriptures, are agreed as to the certainty of this event. But there is a variety of views as to the time and manner of its coming to pass.

Some hold that it is to be preceded and inaugurated by the personal and literal coming of Jesus Christ to reign on the earth. Others believe that it is to be followed by a sudden and desperate revival of wickedness, and that then the second coming of Christ will take place, and the period of final judgment begin; after which, the former constitution of the earth having passed away, the "new heavens and the new earth," the final and eternal abode of redeemed man, shall be established. Others again, make the Millennial period and the "new heaven and the new earth" the same. Without inquiring, now, which of these is the true view, we know this for a certainty—that the period itself has not come. For it would be a mockery of all right interpretation of language, to apply the prophetical descriptions of the Millennial era to any period of human history in the past. But is it near? In the order of events of the future, given us by St. John and Daniel, it comes immediately after the completed outpouring of the seventh vial, under the seventh trumpet. The simple question then for us to decide is,—have all the events described as coming to pass under the sounding of the seventh trumpet been fully realized in history? What these events are, you will find described under the seven vials, for they record more fully the "third woe."

If all the events thus described, have passed into history, it is strange that no one has as yet been able to identify them. And until they are pointed out, we have a right to say that the predictions are as yet, unfulfilled prophecy. Naturally there will be about unfulfilled prophecy much obscurity—many things which we cannot understand until the event comes to pass. But still some great leading facts will stand out so clearly, that we cannot mistake the general course of the prophecy. In this case, there are among others, two events which as it seems to me, are plainly placed between us and the Millennial time.

I. The first is the restoration of the Jews, and their conversion to Christianity. I have already pointed out to you the reasons for the belief in their ultimate return to the land of their fathers. These reasons are found in the oath and covenant of Jehovah with them. But their return is to precede their conversion according to the prophecy. Zechariah, describing their return, says, and I will pour upon the house of David, and upon the inhabitants of Jerusalem, the spirit of grace and supplication; and they shall look upon me whom they have pierced, and they shall mourn for him as one mourneth for his only son." Zech. 12: 10.

Hear also, the plain language of Jesus Christ. After upbraiding the Jews for their unbelief, and foretelling the fearful judgment that was to come upon them, He cries—"Behold your house is left unto you desolate, for I say unto you, ye shall not see me henceforth till ye shall say, Blessed is he that cometh in the name of the Lord." Math. 23: 39. Surely, this implies that the time is coming when they shall hail his messengers as bearers of good news. The language of the apostle Paul is equally explicit and significant,—"and they also, (the Jews) if they abide not still in unbelief, shall be graffed in: for God is able to graff them in again. For if thou (the Gentile) wert cut out of the olive tree which is wild by nature, and wert graffed contrary to nature into a good olive tree; how much more shall these (the Jews) which be the natural branches be graffed into their own olive tree? For I would not, brethren, that ye should be ignorant of this mystery, (the rejection of the Jews for a time) lest ye should be wise in your own conceits, that blindness in part is happened to Israel until the fulness of the Gentiles be come in. And so all Israel shall be saved, as it is written. There shall come out of Zion the Deliverer, and shall turn away ungodliness from Jacob. For this is my covenant unto them when I shall take away their sins." Rom. 11: 23-27. If language can express any positive meaning, surely this declares, that "God hath not cast away His people which He foreknew," but that the time is coming when they, so marvelously preserved among the nations, shall own the King they once rejected. On this event also,—the restoration of the Jews to their covenant privileges—depends the complete triumph of Christianity. This is what Paul declares—"Now if the fall of them be the riches of the world, and the diminishing of them, the riches of the Gentiles, how much more their fulness? If the casting away of them be the reconciling of the world, what shall the receiving of them be but life from the dead?" Rom. 11: 12-15. Great indeed is the indebtedness of the Gentile world to the Jew. We are the heirs of his riches, greater than all we have received from the people of Egypt and Assyria, of Greece and Rome. That old Book full of the records of the chosen people, has done far more for us than Homer's songs, or the classic pages of Heroditus and Thucydides. Better far than Grecian culture, are Israel's laws. For us David still sings the matchless songs of Zion, and Isaiah utters the entreaties and warnings of the living God. From the Jew we have received the language and imagery that express our highest and noblest conception of spiritual things. His cries of old are the models for our prayers; his ritual the best symbol of our spiritual life. The names of his mountains express our souls' elevation or fears: his river marks the boundary of our mortal life, and the name of his chief city tells us of our everlasting home. Of the Jew we have received patriarchs and kings, grander than all the heroes of Greece and Rome, the men of royal lives who still show us how true greatness is to be won. And more than all, from the Jew "as concerning the flesh, Christ came, who is over all, God blessed forever."

But there is a sad break in his history. For eighteen centuries he has done nothing for the world. He has lived in exile—not a leader or a teacher among men. The only notable exceptions to this rule are those who have renounced Judæism for Christianity. But a better day is coming. The Apostle assures us that the world will receive an additional blessing from the Jew through his conversion. "What shall the receiving of them be but life from the dead!" It will be like a glorious resurrection, so wonderful will the effect of their conversion be upon the world. This event then, lies between the present and the millennial era; nor judging the future fulfillment of prophecy by the past, is it likely to be brought about in a day. I do not affirm that it is not now in process of fulfillment. It may be so. Certain it is that from some cause or causes, there is an increasing tide of Jews going back to Palestine. Statistics show that in A. D. 1858 there were only 20,000 there; in A. D. 1863, 100,000; and now the number is estimated as high as 200,000. We can readily understand, if the rule of the Moslem were utterly removed from Palestine, and the blessings of a just government carried there, how the process of return would be much more rapid. But there is no hint given that it is to be sudden and in one body like the Exodus. On the contrary, the prophetic type of it is, the return from the Babylonian captivity. Jeremiah describes it in this manner—"Behold, I will send for many fishers, saith the Lord, and they shall fish them; and after, will I send for many hunters, and they shall hunt them from every mountain, and from every hill, and out of the holes of the rocks." The idea here is, that a variety of causes in God's providence shall move them to return. Some are drawn, and some are driven; some caught by this bait and others by that. Singly, or in groups they go. It is then no objection to the belief that the Jews will return to the land of there fathers, because multitudes of them cherish no such desire, or expectation, On the contrary, this is just what the prediction of Jeremiah would lead us to expect. Why should God send "fishers to fish them," and "hunters" to drive them home, if they were ready and waiting as soon as the way was prepared? If you want to find out God's purposes of mercy, do not look to the heart of an unconverted and rebellious man to find them. So if you wish to find out the purposes of his grace concerning his ancient people, do not listen to the cry of their unbelief, but to the testimony of the Divine

Word. Stout hearted they are in their rejection of the gospel truth; who can change them? But it is written,—"God is able to graff them in again." But certain it is that the millennial song will not rise up from this earth, the scene of so many conflicts and wars, until the voice of the Jew joins in the praises of Him who was crucified for man's sins on Calvary's hill.

II. The second event to be fulfilled before the millennial era, is that recorded in Rev. 16: 19-21. It is also described more minutely in the eighteenth chapter. It is the overthrow of that which St. John calls "Babylon the great, the mother of harlots and abominations of the earth." Let me read you the description which the revelator gives of this mysterious power which was to rise up within the Church, and to continue until the millennial time. He designates it as "the great whore that sitteth upon many waters." A lewd woman is the symbol of an idolatrous system or church; the true Church is the bride, the Lamb's wife. The prophets, whose symbolic language John uses, universally call idolatry, lewdness. The angle explains his own language, "He saith unto me, the waters which thou sawest where the whore sitteth, are peoples, and multitudes, and nations, and tongues; and the woman which thou sawest is that great city which reigneth over the kings of the earth." She is described as arrayed in royal apparel, the emblem of sovereignty. "The woman was arrayed in purple and scarlet color, having a golden cup in her hand, full of abominations and filthiness of her fornications," that is, presenting something particularly attractive and seductive to all who approached her, but which after all was deadly and unclean. She is described "as drunken with the blood of the saints, and with the blood of the martyrs of Jesus." Evidently it is a power which rejoiced in persecuting the children of God. Her place of abode is described; "the seven heads are seven mountains, on which the woman sitteth."

Again it is pictured as a power holding many of God's people in some way under its control, for the voice from heaven is—"Come out of her my people, that ye be not partakers of her sins." Paul, in his second letter to the Thessalonians, gives a description of this same power. He calls it, "that man of sin who opposeth and exalteth himself above all that is called God, or that is worshipped; so that he, as God, sitteth in the temple of God, showing himself that he is God." Manifestly, this is the description of some power that claims the prerogatives which God alone can exercise, and that exalts itself above the revealed Word of God. Daniel describes this same power, as growing up in the last days of the Roman empire; as "speaking great words against the most High"—that is, speaking blasphemously against God's honor, and by its utterances proclaiming doctrines contrary to the Divine Word; as "wearing out the saints of the Most High,"—that is, it was to be a persecutor of those who believe in Christ; as "thinking to change times and laws;" it would attempt legislation in religious matters, thus usurping the prerogatives of God. The description of this mysterious power is given at great length, and with much minuteness in the Scriptures: but it is not my purpose to dwell upon it. Whatever it may be, it is to appear, and to reign according to Daniel's prophecy, for a period of 1250 years, and then be destroyed, before the millennial era shall come. Very positive is Paul's language on this point;—"now we beseech you, brethren, by the coming of our Lord Jesus Christ, and by our gathering together unto Him, that ye be not soon shaken in mind, or be troubled neither by spirit, nor by word, nor by letter, as from us, as that the day of Christ is at hand. Let no man deceive you by any means; for that day shall not come, except there come a falling away first, and that man of sin be revealed, the son of perdition; who opposeth and exalteth himself above all that is called God."

"Remember ye not that when I was with you, I told you these things? And now ye know what withholdeth, that he might be revealed in his time. For the mystery of iniquity doth already work; only he who now letteth, will let, until he be taken out of the way; and then shall that wicked be revealed, whom the Lord shall consume with the spirit of his mouth, and shall destroy with the brightness of his coming." II. Thes. 2: 1-8.

Has this power appeared in history? Evidently it is not paganism, for that was before Paul's time. Nor is it Mahometanism; that did not grow up within the church. Some have applied it to certain Roman emperors, but manifestly, incorrectly, for they were all dead more than a thousand years ago, and the millennium has not come. Some have said that it was Lutheranism, and that Luther was Anti-christ. But evidently the description does not apply to him. He never obtained supremacy over the kings of the earth, nor did he live in splendor, nor did he persecute the saints of God, nor did he claim divine powers, nor was his power seated in a great city with seven hills. He never claimed authority to act as God alone has the right to do. As for example, he never asserted the right to a supreme authority over the consciences of men, for God alone is the Lord of the conscience. He never claimed power to forgive sins, and absolve men from guilt, for God alone can forgive sins. He never claimed to be infallible in spiritual truth, for that is God's prerogative. He never made himself greater than God, in that he sold pardons for a price, to sinful men. He never taught that men might worship images, or saints, or departed spirits, and thus led them into idolatrous worship. I freely admit that had he claimed to do all this, and had he acquired rule and authority over the nations and kings of the earth, he would have had the marks described in the prophecy. This "Man of Sin" is described as "working signs, and lying wonders"— that is, claiming miraculous power. The only approximation, or at least the only thing that could possibly be supposed to look toward this in Luther's history, was the claim, that in his ministrations, he could by uttering certain words, mysteriously inclose in a spiritual manner, the Lord of all in a certain portion of bread and wine, and then hand it over to a fellow man to be eaten. But this was only a faint approximation to a greater wonder constantly wrought by others. Would you know what is the great miracle of all history? Many wonders are recorded in the Divine Word, but this in strangeness transcends them all. That was a glorious manifestation of divine power which accompanied the word of Peter when he bade the lame man at the Gate Beautiful, rise and walk. Immediately his ancle bones received strength. But still it was a living man restored to himself. Wonderful was the display of divine power at the grave of Lazarus! Jesus prayed and then commanded the dead man to come forth, and he came. But still it was a dead man that was raised, not a stone or a clod turned into a man. But behold a miracle that overshadows all these! A man lays before him a wafer made of flour. He prays, speaks a sentence, and lo! the flour is turned into a a God—an object that can be worshipped; it is the real body and blood and soul of Him who is enthroned in glory. This, my friends, is the most stupendous of all miracles, or else, "a lying wonder," exercising a delusive power over multitudes.—No, it would so far as the prophecy is concerned, be without a warrant to call Luther, "the man of sin," "Babylon the Great," and "the harlot drunken with the blood of martyrs." If we could find in the history of christendom, some great, controlling idolatrous power, growing up in the church itself, from causes that were working in Paul's time; if we could find it enthroned in some imperial city, reigning over many nations and peoples, bringing kings into alliance with it, and living royally; if we could find within it and under its control, many of God's people, who are called upon "to come out of her;" if we could find this power persecuting the saints of God, and rejoicing over the slaughter of thousands slain on account of their faith in Jesus Christ, as the only mediator; if we could find it speaking and acting as none but God is able to do,—all reasonable and fair minded men would say, that it was the counterpart of that described in the prophecy. But even should you find just such a power revealed in history, you must also be able to say that it is already consumed by the Spirit proceeding out of Christ's mouth—that is, wasted away by the light from his Holy Word—before you can assert that the millennial day is at hand. It must be remembered too, that this process of consuming by the Word is a slow one. Error smolders and smokes long in the fires of truth. No, the end is not yet. Doubtless we are nearing the longed-for day. The processes that hasten it are moving with increased speed, as the years go by. We have, indeed, many signs of encouragement, and gleams come that seem to herald the morning. But still we must wait. The chart tells us that many untraveled leagues lie between us and the harbor.

If what I have said be true, then the opinion held by many godly and devoted men and women, that we may expect Christ to appear in the clouds at any moment, is not correct.

If what I have said be the testimony of God's Word, then there remains for all who love the Lord Jesus Christ, and look for his appearing, a time for earnest labor, and patient witness-bearing; for upon the prayers of His people is hinged the fulfillment of his glorious promises with regard to the future. We are to "hasten unto the coming of the Lord," by the faithful and diligent use of the instrumentalities appointed by Him for the establishment of his kingdom. Our Lord has said,—"This gospel of the kingdom shall be preached in all the world, for a witness unto all nations, and then shall the end come." But to us He has said, "Go ye into all the world and preach the gospel to every creature." Thus are we to hasten the end.

Does the conclusion, that we are not to expect the second coming of our Lord immediately, remove a fear and bring a sense of relief to any? O, glorious Redeemer! and is it so that men for whom thou hast died, that thou mayest exalt them to thine own glory, are relieved to know that thou delayest thy coming! Are these they of whom thou didst speak when thou saidst—"But, and if that evil servant shall say in his heart my Lord delayeth his coming, and shall begin to smite his fellow-servants, and to eat and drink with the drunken, the lord of that servant shall come in a day when he looketh not for him, and in an hour that he is not aware of, and shall cut him asunder, and appoint his portion with the hypocrites. There shall be weeping and gnashing of teeth?" Yes, there is "a coming of Christ," that may surprise us any moment. We know not what moment we may stand in His presence. But with what sad and terrible surprise must it come to the faithless and unbelieving man, who refused to stand as a witness for Christ's grace, and a worker in his cause!

Lecture VI.

The Millennial Era.

[Rev. 20: 1-7.]

AND I saw an angel come down from heaven, having the key of the bottomless pit and a great chain in his hand.

2 And he laid hold on the dragon, that old serpent, which is the Devil, and Satan, and bound him a thousand years.

3 And cast him into the bottomless pit, and shut him up, and set a seal upon him, that he should deceive the nations no more, till the thousand years should be fulfilled: and after that he must be loosed a little season.

4 And I saw thrones, and they sat upon them, and judgment was given unto them: and *I saw* the souls of them that were beheaded for the witness of Jesus, and for the word of God, and which had not worshipped the beast, neither his image, neither had received *his* mark upon their foreheads, or in their hands; and they lived and reigned with Christ a thousand years.

5 But the rest of the dead lived not again until the thousand years were finished. This *is* the first resurrection.

6 Blessed and holy *is* he that hath part in the first resurrection: on such the second death hath no power, but they shall be priests of God and of Christ, and shall reign with him a thousand years.

7 And when the thousand years are expired, Satan shall be loosed out of his prison.

THE Scriptures, as we have already seen, predict the coming of a time when the kingdoms of this world shall become the kingdoms of our Lord and of his Christ.

The gospel is destined to exercise a wider and more glorious control over the affairs of this world, than has as yet been manifested in history. Somewhere in the future lies a bright and happy period when the true Church of God, having passed through the time of judgment and conflict, and embracing without distinction both Jew and Gentile in its fellowship, shall be the ruling power in the earth. Nations will be christian; and laws and government be molded and guided by the spirit of the gospel. Men of Christlike mind shall rule, and the kingdoms of the earth, no longer hostile, shall minister to the cause of Christ. Ignorance and superstition, oppression and misrule with their attendant ills, shall disappear, and the rule of which the angels sang when their joyful chorus proclaimed, "on earth peace, good will to men," shall be established in glorious power. This period, according to the plain sense of the Scriptures, lies somewhere between the present time and "the end." It is not to be confounded with the era of eternal glory, which is to come after the end of the world and the final judgment. In other words, it is not heaven, but a triumph of Christ's kingdom on earth. The prophets speak of it in language which while highly figurative and obscure in many respects, still leaves the the deep and positive impression upon the reader, that such a time is sure to come. The belief that it is coming, is a deep-seated one in the heart of the waiting Church. It has always made her confident of ultimate triumph, and earnest in her labors. It moves her to pray in confidence, "Thy kingdom come." It lives in her gladdest songs. All believers sing as in one grand chorus—

THE MILLENNIAL ERA. 97

"Behold the mountain of the Lord
  In latter days shall rise,
On mountain tops above the hills,
  And draw the wondering eyes.

The beams that shine from Zion's hill
  Shall lighten every land;
The King who reigns in Salem's towers
  Shall all the world command.

No strife shall vex Messiah's reign
  Or mar the peaceful years,
To plow shares men shall beat their swords,
  To pruning-hooks their spears."

In this twentieth chapter of the Revelation, we find the most minute account which the New Testament gives of the period commonly called the Millennium. A careful comparison of the description given by St. John of this event, and that recorded by Daniel in the seventh chapter of his prophecies, will show that both prophets agree as to the time and manner of its coming to pass. Daniel proclaims that after the destruction of "the fourth beast," that is, the last of the hostile kingdoms of the world, and of the "anti-Christ," then "the kingdom and the dominion and the greatness of the kingdom under the whole heaven, shall be given to the people of the saints of the Most High, whose kingdom is an everlasting kingdom and all dominions (lit. rulers) shall serve and obey Him. Dan. 7: 27. In like manner St. John, after recording the overthrow of the mystical Babylon, the type of an apostate church (Rev. 18), and the destruction of "the beast" and the false prophet (Rev. 19: 19-21), announces the reign of

Christ. The old and hostile powers having been destroyed, new "thrones" are set up, and judgment and rule given to them. Their occupants are the same as those described by Daniel. This much is not only plain from the Word of God, but it finds its confirmation in the facts of history. We all know that if the gospel, by its holy principles, is to reign supreme among the affairs of men, there must be a mighty shaking and overturning of the present order of things. Nothing short of the absolute destruction of many things that now exist, and the reconstruction and remodeling of both Church and State, in many important respects, could make such a rule possible. Take our own system of free government, of which we boast as being conformable to the teachings of the gospel, and who will dare say that either in its laws, or in their administration, it gives us a true embodiment of the great principles of justice and truth, of liberty and law taught in this Word? It would be a mockery of our best and brightest hopes for the future to say that the language of prophecy concerning the gospel dispensation on earth meant no more, and that the gospel itself could do no more for society than is now realized. No, the mission of the gospel, as "a sword," is not yet exhausted. Still the Rider on the white horse, whose name is "Faithful and True," and who "in righteousness doth judge and make war," must go forth on his mission of overturning and conquest. Still, "out of his mouth" must issue "the sharp sword to smite the nations." It is the Divine Word, "which is quick and powerful and sharper than any two-edged sword," which is to smite everything that makes war against the

Rider and opposes his kingdom. Its mission through the ministration of the Holy Spirit, is to prepare the way for the empire of Peace. Thus, the present condition of the world confirms the testimony of prophecy, by proclaiming the necessity of those very changes and overturnings which prophecy said should be made in the last days, before the full triumph of the Gospel. And furthermore, we can see from history that if the process so beautifully described in the vision of the Rider on the white horse, (Rev. 19: 11-21) is carried on in the future as it has been in the past, it must end in the complete overthrow of all those powers typified by "the beast," and "the false prophet," and "the harlot." What is the testimony of the history of the past four hundred years, since the Word of God has gone forth freely among the nations? To say that it has not dispelled ignorance and superstition—that it has not broken the power of secular and ecclesiastical despotism—that it has not removed oppression and revolutionized society for the better, is to falsify the facts of history. What glorious conquests has it already made! The "beastly" powers of the earth do indeed still make war against it; but let the same process of progress and triumph continue, and every candid reader of history must say that all opposition is doomed to that terrible overthrow predicted by St. John. I have alluded to the time and manner of the coming of the millenial era, because it has been strenuously urged by some, that it is to be preceded and inaugurated by the personal and visible coming of the Lord Jesus, to reign on the earth.

In their view, the means now used for the evangelization of the earth are not sufficient to bring about the millennial time. So far as the great result is concerned, they are a failure. Dr. Cumming, of London, a distinguished representative of this class, says: "Many pious people think that all that is required to usher in the sunshine of the millennial day is to improve the Church, to renovate the State, circulate the Bible, and disseminate tracts; and that the result of this will be a millennial condition such as the world has never reached. I do not believe in ultimate victory by any or all of these things." Again he says: "We are looking for Christ and not the mere spread of Christianity." All this is simply a disparagement of the means appointed and blest by the great Head of the Church for the extension of his kingdom, and the conversion of men. The gospel nowhere teaches that the personal advent of Christ, in the glory of the second coming, is to convert the world. The splendor of his appearing will, indeed, fill sinners with fear, terror and despair, but it will not add one to the number of those who already believe. In the description which St. John gives of the causes which bring about the complete overthrow of the kingdoms of the world, and of the false prophet, we search in vain for any thing that indicates the visible appearance of the Lord Jesus. There is indeed a special manifestation of divine power, other than that proceeding from the Word and the ministry of the Holy Ghost, which secures the establishment of millennial peace; but it is one exerted, not on men, but on Satan, the great adversary. The Word of God is a revelation for men, not for devils; so after it has accomplished its mission of revolutionizing the world and casting down its hostile powers, another and a different agency is described as restraining the adversary who worked through men, and who raised up and animated "the beast" and "the false prophet." It is simply an act of sovereign power by which Satan is "bound." The power of the "Prince of this world" is restrained. We may fairly conclude from the description, that the angel or messenger who does this is none other than the Lord Jesus himself. At least it is a power direct from heaven that binds the great destroyer, who has hitherto been permitted to exercise his wiles on the children of men. It is one who carries in his hands the emblem of powers which belong exclusively to the Lord. It is the enthroned "Son of Man," who says in the beginning of the revelations, "I am he that liveth and was dead: and behold I am alive for evermore, Amen; and have the keys of hell and death." (Rev. 1: 18.) These keys He may intrust to a messenger; but the power they represent is His. But evidently the whole transaction here described is a spiritual one. We must not think of literal chains holding a spirit, or of its confinement with visible locks and seals. The meaning manifestly is, that by a direct exercise of divine power, Satan shall be so restrained that he shall not, as hitherto, be able to deceive the nations of the earth. Two causes, then, according to St. John, prepare the way for the establishment of the millennial era: the word of God, operating upon men through the ministration of the Spirit, and the power of God in restraining the power of Satan. If, as some claim, the visible coming of Christ is the chief cause, how strange that the Revelator omitted it altogether:

But what does the Millennium imply? What is to come to pass during the "thousand years?" Here it becomes us to speak with caution. Multitudes give reign to their fancy, and speak with confidence of the details of that coming time, as though they were eye-witnesses of its glory. It is not strange that it should be so, for it is much easier to expound unfulfilled prophecy, provided the day of fulfillment is postponed long enough, than it is to apply fulfilled prophecy. Jesus Christ said to those who accused him in their hearts of blasphemy, because he assumed to forgive the sins of the man who was lying helpless before him, "Which is easier to say, Thy sins be forgiven thee, or to say, Arise and walk?" Evidently it was easier for one having divine power to say "Thy sins be forgiven thee," for if a pretender, only the issue of the judgment day could prove that he had no power. But if he said to a helpless paralytic, "Arise now and walk," the immediate result would be the test of his power. So if one expounds fulfilled prophecy, he must have a care lest another confront him with the facts of history, and prove him ignorant or mistaken. But much easier is it for him to dogmatize concerning the prediction of events a thousand years to come, for who can prove him false by confronting him with the reality? Instead, then, of attempting to speculate, and appealing to the future for the truth of our fancies, let us consider honestly the testimony of this Word. It is on the passage before us, (Rev. 30: 1-7) that the doctrine of the millenium, as such is founded. The language employed by the revelator is highly figurative, and much of it is obscure. We can, therefore, put a great variety of meaning into it, but if we would be honest interpreters, we must be careful to draw out of it that only which agrees with the general teachings of the Scriptures, especially remembering the wise rule, that we are to interpret what is obscure in the light of that which is plain.

1. We learn from this prophecy, that the millennium is to be a time when the power of evil is to be greatly limited and restrained. As already intimated, the great agencies through which Satan hitherto wrought to deceive and destroy men having been cast down, he will not be permitted to raise up new ones. Ignorance and superstition, licentiousness and intemperance, war and misrule, skepticism and atheism, shall no longer be the satanic instruments for the destruction of countless thousands of the race. There was a time, described in these visions, when Satan seemed to reign supreme; but in the new age, the very reverse is to come to pass. We are not, however, to understand that during this period the power of evil is completely destroyed. It is only "bound" for a period, and afterwards breaks forth with peculiar violence. Evil will still be in the world. There is no intimation that human nature will not be the same then as now, needing divine grace to convert and sanctify it; unless, indeed, we accept the view held by some, that the "resurrection" spoken of is a literal one, by which human nature is glorified. The scene of the vision is still "on earth," with its nations exposed to temptation and sin.

2. It is to be the time of a new rule or authority in society; a time when righteous men shall have the supreme control. "*And I saw thrones, and they sat upon*

them." It is not said who sat upon them, but we can fairly gather from what follows that the occupants of the "thrones," the emblems of supreme power, are those described as if they had been martyrs beheaded for the witness of Jesus, and had not in any way yielded themselves servants to the power of the god of this world. In the sixth verse they are described as the fruits of "*the first resurrection.*" They are "*the priests of God and of Christ,*" and "*they shall reign with him a thousand years.*" Whatever may be taught by this language, one thing is certain—it presents us with a picture of the world the very reverse of that drawn by the same hand, of its condition previous to the millennial time. One of the accusations brought against the first missionaries of the Gospel was, "These that have turned the world upside down are come hither," And here, as an effect of the Gospel, we have the picture of the world "upside down," but after all with the right side up. Formerly Satan was unbound and raging like a lion, seeking whom he might devour; but now he is bound. In the old order, the kings of the earth, influenced and controlled by the "beast," and the dragon, and the false prophet, ruled; but now they are "cast down," and new "thrones" are set up. In the former age, St. John saw "the souls of them that were slain for the word of God, and for the testimony which they held;" but then they were "under the altar"—that is, in the place of sacrifice and supplication, crying "with a loud voice," as in agony and trouble, "How long Oh Lord, holy and true, dost Thou not judge and avenge our blood on them that dwell on the earth?"—[Rev. 6: 10.] But now he sees these same souls no longer in trouble and sorrow, but enthroned and ruling in the very world where they were slain. Formerly those who would not worship the beast were killed, and "no man might buy or sell, save he that had the mark of the beast." [Rev. 13: 15-17.] Their condition was one of danger and bondages. But now they are to sit on "thrones," they are "to live and reign."

Imagine a condition of society in which men like Paul and Peter, like Huss and Luther, like Knox and Wesley—I mean, like them, not in their imperfections, but in their bold, outspoken and unfaltering attachment to the truth as it is in Jesus—are to be the rulers and leaders; imagine a state in which those men who have refused to yield either their "heads" or their "hands" as the instruments of unrighteousness, are chief in honor and power; in short, a condition in which the power of evil shall not only be in its minimum, but in which it shall seem as if all the noblest spirits of the past, the men who were boldest, most outspoken, zealous and uncompromising in the service of Christ, were alive, and controlling human affairs in accordance with the mind and will of Christ, and you will have the spiritual reality which this prophecy describes. If this be what the revelator means in general, his description accords precisely with the plain testimony of Scripture.

Daniel says, "The people of the saints of the most High" shall possess the kingdom. "In His days," writes the Psalmist, "shall the righteous flourish." "Yea, all kings shall fall down before Him; all nations shall serve Him." "The meek shall inherit the earth."

Thus far you will agree with me, whatever interpretation you may hold of other parts of the language here used. But, you ask, does it not mean much more? Is there not some new and supernatural element characterizing this promised era, which we do not and cannot realize in society as now constituted? Undoubtedly this language, as well as that used elsewhere in the Scriptures, implies something more than a general and widespread knowledge of the Gospel, and the consequent elevation of society, and the infusion of a better spirit into existing governments, both in Church and State. A fair interpretation of it in the connection in which it stands, demands a remodeling of society, the destruction of much that remains, and the rebuilding according to a new rule. The change from the present to that blessed period of triumph and peace, involves a shaking of earthly things to their foundations, "that those things which can not be shaken," the things of God, may "remain." It is not possible for us to tell accurately, what will be the state of affairs in this world when every thing comes under the power and direction of a living, practical Christianity. As the carnal element, the "beastial" power of the world, is utterly overthrown, and the spiritual element gains the ascendency over human affairs, who can tell what new powers will be developed among men; what new beauty the race will put on, and how it shall seem as if the world had undergone a resurrection? The blessing promised to men through the Holy Spirit, has not yet been exhausted, and when in that day it shall come in all its wonderful fullness, it would not be strange that changes should be wrought in society, and in man's relation to the unseen world, of which we can not now conceive.

The Scriptures give us hints of physical changes in nature that aid to make this coming era:

"The earth shall yield her increase." "It shall be fat and plenteous." "The wilderness shall be a fruitful field." "The wilderness and the solitary places shall be glad for him, and the desert shall rejoice and blossom as the rose." It is true that these are chiefly poetical expressions representing the joy of nature, so long cursed by man's sins, in the sunny time of peace. But we can readily see that, with the cessation of desolating wars, and the removal of oppression, and with the right direction of labor and capital, hitherto wasted, "showers of blessings" upon the earth would follow. The earth shows no sign of exhaustion, nor has man, as yet, found out a tithe of the riches of material treasures God has prepared for him in this world. The future will bring more wonderful inventions and discoveries than any in the past. Think for a moment that the past one hundred years have brought to us most of the discoveries of modern times, the inventions that characterize our age, and that have, in a sense, revolutionized society. What may we not, then, expect from a future in which the conditions of development will be vastly more favorable?

But is there not something more than all this? Are we not to expect the companionship of risen and glorfied men; and above all, in that glad period, will not Christ himself appear in his glory to dwell among men? There is indeed, a time when Christ shall dwell visibly among his people, when they "shall see his face," and be like him. That time is described by St. John in the last two chapters of the Revelation. But in the order observed by him, it is after the Millennium. In this description of the millennial time, there is not the slightest hint given of His dwelling on the earth, unless it is in the expression, "they reigned with Christ a thousand years." Surely that is a very vague and shadowy ground upon which to base a doctrine that is not taught elsewhere in the Scriptures, in plain literal statements. How strange that St. John should have omitted from his description of the millennial time, that which, if true, would have been its chief and crowning feature—the visible presence of the Lord Jesus! He dwells lovingly upon that fact as constituting the chief glory of heaven, but he has nothing to say concerning it, in describing the time when, according to some interpreters, Christ is to dwell on the earth a thousand years. Many have based upon the language here used by the revelator, the belief that Christ will come to reign visibly upon the earth; that He will establish Himself as the head of a visible, external kingdom; and that when He comes, the martyrs, or, as others believe, all who sleep in Jesus, shall be raised from the dead and reign with Him in His earthly kingdom; and after this reign of one thousand years, the general resurrection, and final judgment will take place. This, with many modifications as to details, is what is known as the Pre-millennial advent theory. It is not to be denied that it has been held and advocated by many men, eminent for piety and biblical learning, from the days of Irenaeus and Tertullian to the present time. But while many things may be said in its favor, it is after all, a theory which finds its chief support from the literal application of what is plainly, highly figurative and symbolical language. It is not only unsupported by the plainer parts of Scripture, but it is in positive contradiction to many of its statements. Time will not permit me to point out these contradictions. I can only show you that this passage manifestly, does not assert the literal resurrection of the martyrs. or the visible reign of Christ. St. John tells us that he saw the "*souls*" of the martyrs—not their risen and glorified bodies. There is not the slightest hint given of so wonderful a fact as the resurrection of their bodies from their graves. Their souls live and reign—that is all. Admitting for a moment that this passage asserts their resurrection, then we are shut up to the conclusion that the martyrs alone are raised from the dead in "the first resurrection," and that they are to rule on the earth with Christ. All this is contrary to the plain testimony of St. Paul, who tells us that when Christ comes the second time, all the dead in Christ shall rise first; that is, before the wicked; that those who are alive and believe on him shall be changed and caught up into the air to meet the Lord, and so be forever with the Lord.

Nor can we understand "the first resurrection" of which St. John speaks, to be that "rising first" from the dead, of which St. Paul speaks. The time is not the same, nor are the effects the same. St. John's description of the resurrection of the dead is given further on. (Rev. 20: 11-14.) and as occurring long after this. And furthermore, that description accords perfectly with what Paul, and our Lord himself say about that great event. This "first resurrection," is evidently a symbolical one, descriptive of some great fact or condition in the millennial time. Now, what great characteristic fact in christian experience is there which would be scripturally symbolized by "a resurrection," and which would specially belong to the people of the millennial time? Happily, the Word of God furnishes the answer. It is regeneration. Hear the language of scripture concerning this great fact. "Verily, verily, I say unto you, except a man be born again, he cannot see the kingdom of God." "Verily, verily, I say unto you, he that heareth my words and believeth on Him that sent me, hath everlasting life, and shall not come into condemnation, but is passed from death unto life." John 5: 24. "And you hath He quickened who were dead in trespasses and sins. * * But God, who is rich in mercy, for his great love wherewith he loved us, even when we were dead in sins, hath quickened us together with Christ, and hath raised us up together and made us to sit together in heavenly places in Jesus Christ." Eph. 2: 1-4-6. "If ye then be risen with Christ, seek those things which are above." Col. 3: 1. Is not this that great change which can truly be called the "first resurrection?" Its effects are just those which St. John describes, "*Over such the second death hath no power.*" So Jesus testifies concerning his believing and regenerated people,—"they have everlasting life, and shall not come into condemnation." "*They shall be priests of God and of Christ.*" So it is written of those who are "born again," "ye also, as lively stones, are built up a spiritual house, an holy priesthood." "Ye are a chosen generation, a royal priesthood." Who are "*blessed and holy*" among the children of men save those who have been renewed and sanctified by the Holy Ghost? It is to such that the

Word of God gives these titles. Now, remembering that St. John is here giving the picture of "a world turned upside down" by the gospel, how significant is his application of this term, "the first resurrection." Before, it was an unregenerated world, in which the vast multitudes were dead in trespasses and sins, and only a few lived. Now, the overwhelming multitudes are alive in Christ and only a few, the remainder, are dead. What wonder that in beholding a glad society of regenerated men, he should write, "This is the first resurrection." Behold these blessed and holy men! They have eternal life; over them the second death hath no power; they are kings and priests unto the Lord forever. There is much more that I would like to say concerning the characteristics and the duration of this period, and the events to follow it, but time forbids me. From what has been said you can see that the glories of this coming time, are spiritual rather than material. They are not the splendors of outward estate or worldly abundance, but of minds and hearts, enlightened, renewed, and sanctified by the grace of God. It is a triumphant spiritual kingdom in the world, but not of the world.

If this be the true scriptural view, we can readily be sharers in what is the chief and essential blessing of that glad time. We can even now "see the kingdom of God." "Blessed and holy is he that hath part in the first resurrection." Yes, blessed is he who, by faith in Christ, has passed from death unto life, no matter whether he lives now or in the ages that shall witness the largest triumphs of the gospel. Were that glad time to begin suddenly, were it to break in noonday splendor upon the world with the sunrise of the coming morning, it could not make you blessed unless you were born again. No coming of Christ in outward splendor; no glory of a transformed earth made beauteous with more than Eden's greenness, can ever make a sinful, unbelieving heart happy, or turn it from death unto life. Would you have part in the millennial joys? would you be among that blessed number who shall rejoice in the triumph and reign of Christ? Then you must have part in "the first resurrection."

This view also gives us occasion for great rejoicing as we look toward the future. It is full of hope and blessedness for the race of man, and full of triumph for the cause of Christ. We look not only for the coming of the Savior, but also for the spread of His gospel, until He shall have an innumerable seed to serve Him. The issue of the great work of redemption will not be seen in a little remnant saved, and in overwhelming multitudes lost; but in a "great multitude" that no man can number, saved eternally, by the grace of God. The Millennium will be a time of abundant sowing and reaping. The earth shall yield her increase in a glad harvest of souls, and the Redeemer of men shall see of the travail of His soul and be satisfied.

www.ingramcontent.com/pod-product-compliance
Lightning Source LLC
Chambersburg PA
CBHW020143170426
43199CB00010B/861